# Creating
# Award-
# Winning
# History
# Fair Projects

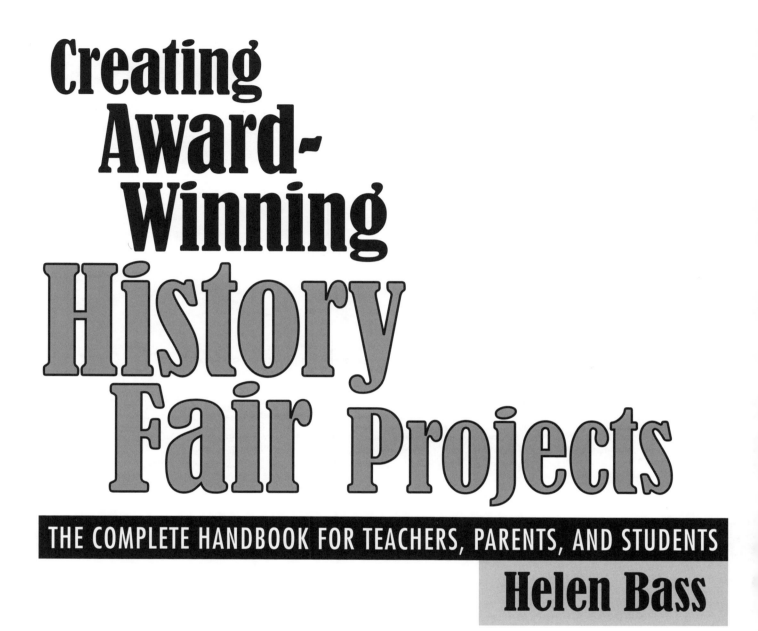

# Creating Award-Winning History Fair Projects

## THE COMPLETE HANDBOOK FOR TEACHERS, PARENTS, AND STUDENTS

### Helen Bass

PRUFROCK PRESS INC.
WACO, TEXAS

Library of Congress Cataloging-in-Publication Data

Bass, Helen.
  Creating award-winning history fair projects : the complete handbook for teachers, parents, and students /
Helen Bass.
     p. cm.
  Includes bibliographical references.
  ISBN-13: 978-1-59363-236-6 (pbk.)
  ISBN-10: 1-59363-236-3 (pbk.)
  1. History—Exhibitions—Handbooks, manuals, etc. 2. History—Study and teaching—Activity programs—
Handbooks, manuals, etc. 3. History—Research—Handbooks, manuals, etc. 4. Fairs—Handbooks, manuals,
etc. I. Title.
  D16.2.B32 2007
  907.1'2—dc22
                              2007025239

ISBN-13: 978-1-59363-236-6
ISBN-10: 1-59363-236-3

Printed in the USA.

At the time of this book's publication, all facts and figures cited are the most current available; all telephone
numbers, addresses, and Web site URLs are accurate and active; all publications, organizations, Web sites,
and other resources exist as described in this book; and all have been verified. The authors and Prufrock Press
make no warranty or guarantee concerning the information and materials given out by organizations or content found at Web sites, and we are not responsible for any changes that occur after this book's publication. If
you find an error or believe that a resource listed here is not as described, please contact Prufrock Press.

Prufrock Press Inc.
P.O. Box 8813
Waco, TX 76714-8813
Phone: (800) 998-2208
Fax: (800) 240-0333
http://www.prufrock.com

To my husband, Joel, for his love and support.

# Contents

# Acknowledgments

Though teachers are the audience of this book, students are the focus, and I deeply appreciate their assistance. The following students contributed their comments and references to this work: Whitney Gafford, David Miller, DeLisa Gross, Jamie Felkner, Sarah Silfer, Evan Wilson, Beka Ray, P. J. Ray, Jesús Hernández, José Mercado, Hector Urquidi, Jessica Diaz, Brenda Muñiz, Roshan Govindbhai, Rachael Arthur, Mayra Muñoz, Daisy Acosta, Judy Acosta, and Carolina Ramírez.

Teachers Luisa Castillo, Chris Terrill, and Donna Patton, as well as librarian Julie Greene, have made valuable contributions to my knowledge and understanding of the wonderful contribution of history fairs to students, faculties, and communities.

Parents are remarkable supporters of their children as they work on their projects. I appreciate input from Stacy Felkner and Allen and Karen Gafford. Karen answered my many questions and provided a superb example of how parents can become involved in the history fair process.

I greatly appreciate the time and expertise Dr. James Olson gave me concerning a historian's perspective on research and creating projects. I am also grateful to my friend, Kay Reynolds, for sharing her childhood polio experience and for encouraging me during the course of writing this book. My daughter-in-law, Sarah Bass, was especially helpful with her advice about scrapbooks.

My husband, Joel, provided valuable feedback to my ideas. Although his field is science, he is also appreciates history. I am especially grateful for his encouragement and support as I worked on researching and writing this book.

All of these people contributed to my efforts to help students, teachers, and parents become successful participants in the amazing adventure of history fairs.

# Introduction

**B**eing involved in a history fair or festival is fun and exciting for everyone involved: students, teachers, parents, and the community. Because history fairs are public displays, they offer students the opportunity to demonstrate their knowledge and understanding of history to a wide audience. The history fair process offers teachers a means of helping their students use their unique talents and intellectual skills to develop historical understanding and a deep appreciation for people of the past. Parents enjoy the prospect of sharing an academic experience with their children, and the community benefits from history fairs by connecting with their local schools. History fairs show student work through exhibits, scrapbooks, posters, models, dioramas, computer and video presentations, or performances of plays, demonstrations, mock trials, and speeches. The events can be on a small, medium, or grand scale. They can be competitive or noncompetitive. They can begin on a local level and advance to district, state, and even national levels, or they can be for a specific occasion at a local school. But, whatever the magnitude of a history fair, they all have these elements in common: They reflect students' deep understanding of historical matters, and they are public, lively, and fun! This book will help teachers and students in grades 6–12 prepare for and conduct history fairs, using a method I have developed called CATCH: Capture a Time, Capture History.

## Capture a Time

Using the methods of historians, students write a historical paper once they select and research a topic, develop a premise, identify points that support that premise, and draw a conclusion. To capture the time of the topic, students explain the historical framework and historical significance of their topics. The historical framework of an event includes the prevailing issues and ideas among the people who lived during the time the event took place. It also includes pertinent geographic factors and influences, as well as societal and cultural issues. The historical significance of an event refers to how the event has made an impact over time. Like historians, students balance their writing by using an appropriate blend of primary and secondary sources and by presenting various points of view from people involved in the events of their topics.

# Capture History

Students follow up their writing by creating a visual project that reflects the historical paper they have written. For example, if a student writes about the significance of Roman law, he or she might create an exhibit showing how Roman laws have influenced societies over time. Or, if a student writes about the way of life in a typical New England colony, he or she might construct a diorama of a Colonial village to illustrate descriptions made in the historical paper. Projects can take the form of performances such as plays, speeches, monologues, storytelling, virtual historical trials, and reenactments. Other projects include media presentations, dioramas, models, exhibits, posters, and scrapbooks.

Creating visual projects also follows the methods of historians and people in professions related to the history field. They base their visual work on the historical framework and historical significance of their spheres of study. Archaeologists draw conclusions about their findings in the field based on a deep knowledge of the people who once occupied a certain site. Curators and museum staff construct models, dioramas, and exhibits based on their understanding of the people and events their displays represent. Filmmakers who make historically accurate movies and documentaries present their work from research and a full understanding of their subject. Actors also deeply study the people they portray in these films. Reenactors, such as mountain men at a rendezvous or soldiers in a staged battle of the past, must also understand the historical framework and historical significance of their event.

This book discusses these components of CATCH in detail and also describes and gives examples of conducting history fairs and festivals that give students the opportunity to present their creations about the past to the public.

# A Teacher's Guide to History Projects

**W**atching students develop their understanding of history is an exciting prospect for teachers. It is also rewarding to realize that, as a teacher, you play a key role in that development. Assisting students in creating and presenting history projects is one of the most effective ways to track individuals as they gain expertise in an area of history that was originally unknown to them. This chapter offers guidelines for helping students design and carry out projects from a historian's standpoint. Two major steps are involved in the CATCH approach: writing a historical paper and creating a visual product reflecting that paper for public display in history events such as fairs, festivals, and exhibitions.

Several other designs are currently in place for history fairs. For example, National History Day is a contest for students in grades 6–12. This program begins in a local school setting and provides for students to move through district, regional, state, and national levels as contest winners advance in their National History Day categories. For more information, see the National History Day Web site at http://www.nationalhistoryday.org.

## How Is CATCH Different From Other Programs?

In this book, the approach to student participation in creating projects designed for public display is different from other programs in several ways. In the CATCH method, students create both a historical paper and a related visual project. The rationale for this design is that students can become thoroughly familiar with a topic by following a historian's method of research in writing a paper, and they can internalize what they learn by becoming personally involved in communicating their understanding through a visual product of their own creation.

Another way the CATCH style is different is that a contest is optional. Although contests are motivational for many students, they are not always desirable or feasible. You might want to have a different emphasis in your history fair. Sometimes it is difficult to secure judges. Some students feel ill at ease about being part of a competition. This book offers ways to carry out a competition, but the choice is up to you and your students. Perhaps you would like to have part of your fair competitive and part of it composed of simply displaying students' work. Or, you might want to give students the option of competing.

Finally, in the CATCH approach, the categories of visual projects are varied and often contain options within a given a category. It is beneficial for students to have opportunities to express what they have learned in ways that use their particular talents and interests. For this reason, this book offers a wide variety of possible visual projects. However, teachers who hold history fairs often have their students create only one kind of project such as a model or a poster. You may choose to limit or expand your categorical options depending on your resources, time frame, and other considerations that affect your students and circumstances.

These differences in approach to conducting history fairs give students and teachers many possibilities. Hopefully, as you read about the historical paper and visual projects in the following discussion, you will find a plan that is just exactly right for you and your students.

# The Historical Paper and Visual Project

The primary reason for writing a paper prior to constructing a visual project is that writing provides students an opportunity to engage with historical material in the manner of a historian.

Following a historian's method, students perform preliminary research to gain sufficient information about a topic so that they can pose significant questions. These questions direct students in an inquiry approach to developing a premise, collecting evidence to support their premise, and drawing conclusions about their findings. This process transports students from simply writing a report that they might copy from limited sources to creating a challenging and thoughtful treatment of a significant issue or event. When students write a well-developed paper before creating a visual project, they have a thorough understanding of their subject matter and an appreciation for the people and times surrounding their project.

For example, a student might want to create a model of a sod house as a replica of those built by early settlers in the Kansas and Nebraska territories. Through researching and writing about the lifestyles of the people who built these homes, students become personally acquainted with the motivations and hardships of people of that era. As students gain an appreciation and depth of understanding of the contributions of these people, students can reflect their learning in the details of a model they construct.

Another reason for writing a historical paper before creating a visual project is that by following the guidelines of writing a complex paper, students are able to become familiar with issues of a given era. They gain an understanding of the historical framework and historical significance of a given topic. For example, even though students may focus on the lifestyle of the early settlers on the plains, writing a historical paper helps students see how these settlers fit into the Westward Movement and the prevailing thought of the people of the mid-19th century.

Chapters 3–5 of this book offer a guide for you to give students as they tackle the mechanics of organizing, researching, and writing a historical paper. As you will see when reading these chapters, you will play a vital role in helping students understand how to prepare for research, identify a topic, develop a premise statement, research a topic, organize a historical paper, and write the paper. In these chapters, students learn how to keep a journal as an organizational tool to help them stay on task and to have a place to collect their research notes and other important information.

Students also see the importance of including key elements of historical writing in their papers such as using correct grammar, writing within a historical framework, maintaining historical accuracy, presenting balanced points of view, effectively using primary and secondary sources, developing a solid structure of organization, and emphasizing the historical significance of their topic.

Once students become thoroughly knowledgeable about their topic, they can create visual projects with accuracy and with a reflection of the historical framework of their topic. Chapter 6 offers information about possible projects for students to create that capture the best representation of their topic. The chapter also enumerates important considerations to keep in mind as students construct their products.

This book presents possibilities for writing historical papers and creating visual projects that represent historical topics. As their teacher, you will be able to choose how extensively you want your students to participate in this learning experience. Several factors such as student concerns and curriculum matters associated with public displays of visual projects are important to examine as you decide how you would like to use the CATCH approach.

# Student Concerns

Before you introduce the idea of engaging in CATCH to your students, you might want to address several issues about your students' involvement and about how carrying out this project will affect your curriculum demands.

One of the major considerations regarding your students is whether they should enter a contest. Contests can be both motivational and intimidating for students, so it is often wise to give students a choice of participating in one. If students choose not to enter a contest, you will want to ensure that they are held to the same high standard of work as those who choose to enter. It might be helpful to display their work in the classroom and to check their efforts while still in progress. For example, whether students are part of a contest or not, written pieces of their visual projects need to have correct spelling in titles and explanations.

Another major consideration is arrangement of students. You know your students, so you understand whether they are more productive working in groups or alone. An advantage of working in groups is that students can share the workload of researching a broad topic, and through discussion, narrow the topic to manageable form. Together, they can develop a premise and determine an approach to researching the supporting points for the premise. However, it may be especially difficult for you to determine how students shared their responsibilities equally when writing the paper portion of the project. A workable solution is for individuals within groups to divide tasks for gathering data in research and for fleshing out certain parts of the paper. You might choose to use a chart like the one offered in Figure 1. A sample of how students should complete this chart is provided in Figure 2.

This device not only helps you see who has accepted responsibility for specific tasks, but it also helps students keep their commitments. As students progress in their work, you might want to occasionally consult the chart and ask students to show you the work they have done to date. This practice will assist you in sifting the slackers from the workers.

It is also important for students to equally share responsibility when working together on their visual projects. If they work both inside and outside of class on their products, you will not always see them in action. You might want to use a chart for the visual projects similar to one used for writing historical papers. A project chart and an example of a completed chart can be found in Figures 3 and 4. Even though each student would have specific responsibilities,

# Individual Responsibilities for Group Members

**Historical Paper's Topic:** _____

*Research*

| Name of Student | Ideas to Investigate |
|---|---|
|  |  |
|  |  |
|  |  |
|  |  |

*Writing*

| Name of Student | Ideas to Develop |
|---|---|
|  |  |
|  |  |
|  |  |
|  |  |

**Figure 1.** Individual responsibilities for group members working on a historical paper.

*Note.* Give this tool to each group of students. The students should use this tool to help organize the tasks of the group. Students' names should be written in the lefthand column and each student's task(s) should be written in the righthand column.

# Individual Responsibilities for Group Members

**Historical Paper's Topic:** Bob Hope's Contribution to World War II

*Research*

| Name of Student | Ideas to Investigate |
|---|---|
| Heather | *Ideas and values of the period:* What were the concerns of civilians and military personnel that caused the people to welcome the boost in morale that Bob Hope offered? |
| Reuben | *Geographical influences:* How did entertaining troops in war zones affect the cast and crew of Bob Hope' tours? |
| Carla | *Social issues:* How did Bob Hope's humor relate to the mood and atmosphere of the time? |
| James | *Cultural issues:* How did the songs and skits in Bob Hope's shows connect to their audiences? |

*Writing*

| Name of Student | Ideas to Develop |
|---|---|
| Heather | Work on phrasing the introduction and conclusion to include all of the appropriate elements of the paper. |
| Reuben | *Develop Supporting Point 1:* Bob Hope's commitment to the enterprise of bringing shows to troops in war zones. |
| Carla | *Develop Supporting Point 2:* How Bob Hope's shows affected those he wanted to help. |
| James | *Develop Supporting Point 3:* Results of Bob Hope's efforts. |

**Figure 2.** Completed example of Figure 1.

*Note.* Students can use this sample to complete their own group charts. Make sure to point out that students can share some responsibilities, if they wish.

# Individual Responsibilities for Group Members

**Visual Project's Title:** _____

**Visual Project Medium:** _____

| Name of Student | Preparation Responsibilities |
|---|---|
|  |  |
|  |  |
|  |  |
|  |  |

| Name of Student | Construction and Presentation Responsibilities |
|---|---|
|  |  |
|  |  |
|  |  |
|  |  |

**Figure 3.** Individual responsibilities for group members for a visual project.

_Note._ On this chart, the visual project's title will probably be the same as the title of the historical paper. However, if the visual project has a different emphasis, the project's title might be different. For example, the paper's title might have been "Life on a Nebraska Prairie." The visual project might be narrower, such as "Sod Home of a Typical Prairie Family." The medium section refers to the category of the project, such as exhibit, play, or scrapbook. In the case of the sod home, the medium would be a model.

# Individual Responsibilities for Group Members

**Visual Project's Title:** "The Hope That Bob Brought"

**Visual Project Medium:** Exhibit

| Name of Student | Preparation Responsibilities |
|---|---|
| Heather | Secure exhibit board and fabric and trim for the board. Work with Reuben to capture and print pictures for the exhibit. Be certain that they reflect the content of the historical paper. |
| Reuben | Borrow a record player and records of artists singing songs they sang when touring with Bob Hope during World War II. Work with Heather to capture and print pictures for the exhibit. |
| Carla | Secure a letter her grandfather wrote to her grandmother after he attended a Bob Hope show on a Pacific Island. Make captions and signs for the exhibit. |
| James | Memorize one of Bob Hope's monologues and prepare to present it when the exhibit is on display. Secure an appropriate costume including a golf club to use as Bob Hope did. |

| Name of Student | Construction and Presentation Responsibilities |
|---|---|
| Heather | Work with Carla to mount pictures and captions on background paper. Work with Carla to explain and answer questions about our group's topic during the public event. |
| Reuben | Work with James to attach background material, trim, and exhibit items to the exhibit board. Set up the record player and play appropriate music during the public event. |
| Carla | Work with Heather to mount pictures and captions on background paper. Work with Heather to explain and answer questions about our group's topic during the public event. |
| James | Work with Reuben to attach background material, trim, and exhibit items to the exhibit board. Present monologue to people who gather at our display during the public event. |

**Figure 4.** Completed example of Figure 3.

they would work together on the project's design and give input concerning each other's contributions.

Accessing information for research is another concern you might have for your students. Many schools have ready Internet access for students, but some do not. In some schools, teachers must schedule time for classes to use computers in a schoolwide lab. Others have computers connected to the Internet in the classroom. You may need to require students to perform Internet research outside of class. Even if students do not have computers at home, most of them have access to computers in local libraries.

However, it is important to stress that the Internet is just one source for gathering information. Chapter 4 provides detailed information about accessing resources that yield information from both primary and secondary sources. It is essential for students to have a balanced assortment of sources, even if they are limited.

If you teach fourth or fifth grade, you might be concerned about how you can modify the elements of CATCH for your students. Elementary students can definitely benefit from writing historical papers and creating visual projects that represent the topics of their papers. This learning experience helps students become aware of the importance of knowing and understanding history and of how historians form and communicate historical concepts. Also, the activity prepares students to participate in more complex research and communication when they reach the secondary grade levels. Several modifications that can help younger students accomplish the CATCH approach appear in Table 1.

# Curriculum Concerns

Although the student issues described above require teachers' attention, curriculum concerns also are important considerations for teachers engaging in CATCH.

One of your greatest curriculum concerns is effective use of time. Teachers never have enough time to offer all of the learning opportunities they know will bring about student understanding. Obviously, developing, researching, and writing a historical paper followed by creating a visual project is time consuming. But, many teachers feel that the effort is worth the time because of the benefit to students. The immediate benefit is that CATCH provides students a step-by-step plan to follow for producing quality work that develops their understanding of historical matters and issues. The long-range benefit is that students have the potential for succeeding in college history classes and for becoming in-depth history learners as adults.

## Table 1
## Modifying CATCH for Fourth- and Fifth-Grade Students.

These modifications help younger students manage writing a historical paper and constructing a visual project connected the concepts presented in the paper.

1. Give students a choice of topics rooted in a larger theme. In the secondary grades, students conduct preliminary research and then select a narrow and manageable topic. Explain to your students that they will research a subject within a larger study. For example, the larger theme might be English Colonization of America, and two of the topics might include "William Penn and the Settlement of Pennsylvania" and "John Smith and the Stubborn Settlers of Jamestown."

2. Define a range of research. It is important for students to understand how a balance of research is necessary to present a complete picture of a topic. In the upper grades, students are responsible for determining if they have achieved a suitable balance. Because younger students need more direction, you might assign them to use no more than three Web sites and at least one encyclopedia, two books, and two sources at large such as media articles or interviews they conduct. Also, you might require at least one primary source so that students can begin to become familiar with the characteristics of primary and secondary sources.

3. Provide a structure for writing a historical paper. In the secondary grades, students develop a premise, state the premise in the paper's introduction, develop paragraphs that support the premise, and write a conclusion. It is helpful for students in the elementary grades to become familiar with the concept of a premise, but you might need to develop one for them. For example, you could give them a prompt that would guide their research and writing of the introduction. Students could use the information they acquire in their research to support the assertion made in the prompt and then write a conclusion summarizing their findings. For example, a prompt for the broader topic of "William Penn and the Settlement of Pennsylvania" might be "William Penn and his Quaker settlers made a lasting impact on the colony of Pennsylvania." In addition, for the other sample topic listed above ("John Smith and the Stubborn Settlers of Jamestown"), you might give students a prompt such as "The leadership of John Smith helped make it possible for Jamestown to become England's first successful settlement."

4. Assist students in understanding how their visual projects represent their historical papers. You might want to give them suggestions of how this is accomplished. For example, an exhibit depicting how William Penn and his settlers made an impact on Pennsylvania would directly reflect on this topic, and a play about John Smith and the early Jamestown settlers would show the reluctance of the men to work for survival and how John Smith had to deal with them. Elementary students are usually quite skillful in constructing visual projects.

One way to address the time issue is to assign students some of the work outside of class. You might want to require students to do a large part of their work in class so that you can monitor their progress, but it is also advantageous for students to do much of the work out of class. The nature of some of their work would necessitate time on task away from school anyway, such as gathering information from interviews and visits to libraries and museums.

Another effective use of time is to engage students in work of this magnitude only once a year and in connection with a unit that you usually spend a lot of time on. Timing also could be important. You might want to connect your CATCH assignment with parents' night or a community observance such as the founding of your city or Veterans' Day.

A second curriculum concern is compliance with standards and statewide testing expectations. Most states have standards stating student expectations of content knowledge and skills with statewide tests derived from these standards. Some states rely on the Curriculum Standards for Social Studies from the National Council for the Social Studies or national standards that specifically address history, geography, government and civics, and economics. Writing historical papers and constructing visual projects are effective means of helping students meet these expectations. In this kind of project, students use social studies skills involving acquiring and interpreting data and effectively communicating concepts and information. Students also deeply pursue and probe historical concepts, events, and innovations. The CATCH approach helps students internalize their knowledge and gain understanding about their topics. It also provides a framework for learning about other historical issues and events they will study in the future.

Assessment is another curriculum matter that occupies teachers' attention. In many ways, CATCH serves as a performance task because the students gather information, apply their knowledge and understanding to a new situation, and present their product to an audience. However you choose to use the assignment, both formative and summative assessments are important during the writing and visual product construction phases of this venture. A rubric for grading historical papers is included in Chapter 5 for your use. Chapter 6 includes rubrics for evaluating each type of project.

Several formative evaluations are inherent in the CATCH approach. During the process, you will want to check for student understanding about terminology in association with researching and writing a historical paper. For example, students need to understand and correctly incorporate certain concepts, such as *historical framework* and *historical significance,* into their work. As you teach these concepts, you might want to connect them to a topic that students have already studied such as the Roman Empire or the Spanish conquest of South America. Then, students could apply their prior knowledge when writing their historical papers. The concepts of historical framework and historical significance are defined and applied throughout this book as part of participating in the CATCH process.

Another formative assessment could be to have students write a paragraph or two describing how their historical papers fit into the context of a larger picture. For example, you recently might have completed a unit on World War II. One of your students or a group of students might want to write a historical paper and construct a visual project about Bob Hope's work with troops in the Pacific during the war. Writing a paragraph about how their project fits into the operations of the Pacific Theater during the war would demonstrate their understanding of the connection of their narrow topic to the broader topic of the war.

As a formative assessment, it is important that students begin their visual projects by writing a paragraph explaining how their projects will reflect the concepts presented in their historical papers. This connection is discussed at the beginning of Chapter 6.

One of the most constructive formative assessments is that of student self-assessment. It is necessary to occasionally give students time to reflect on the quality of their products as they progress in their work and also as they polish the writing and assembly of their visual projects. If students are working in groups, they will have each other to provide valuable feedback. If students are working alone, ask them to pair with another student who is also working alone and give them time to reflect on each other's work and offer feedback.

These are some of the formative assessments that will be useful to you for keeping up with students' progress as they advance in their work. They also are useful to the students, because such assessments give the students opportunities to fine-tune their work along the way. Including a summative evaluation is also crucial within the CATCH process.

A summative evaluation assesses the quality of your students' final products. It is important for students to know exactly what you will require of them to create a successful product. Future chapters provide checklists for students to monitor the quality of their progress and rubrics for you to share with your students, as well as use as a gauge for assessing the level of quality in your students' work.

CATCH is a constructive method for learning and understanding historical concepts, events, issues, and people of the past. I hope you enjoy the adventure alongside your students.

# CHAPTER 2

# A Historian's Method

**T**eaching history is exciting because doing so gives you the opportunity to help students understand how the subject weaves together the stories of people of the past and connects them to people of the present day. Everyone is included because everyone is part of history. Through studying history, students gain an awareness of their place in the ongoing march of humankind. When they are born, they step into a world already formed by centuries of people's ideas and actions that have shaped the sphere of life for future generations. An individual's name might not appear in a history book, but what each person thinks and does influences others and makes a difference that will leave its mark forever. This is important for students to know and understand as they make their own marks in the shaping of humanity.

## Helping Students Become Historians

You and your students are about to undertake the experience of CATCH: Capture a Time, Capture History. You will guide students in capturing a time as they research a topic and write a historical paper about people and events during a certain historical period. To capture history, students will create a visual project that reflects the ideas and concepts of their papers. No matter what your students' topics are, they will be learning about people of the past—how they thought, what was important to them, how their environment affected them, and how they affected their environment. Students will see how these people related to other people and how their traditions and customs played a part in what they achieved or failed to achieve. It is important for students to be aware that people of the past were real people, and they need to be represented as accurately as possible. For students to accomplish this representation in their work, they will need to apply methods historians draw on as they uncover the past.

Historians realize that people of the past lived and operated within a framework unique to them. They were influenced by ideas and practices that were often quite different than ours. For example, students may have difficulty understanding and identifying with the life of a young person who had no exposure to video games, computers, movies, telephones, or other electronic devices. He would have spent his time much different than the way young people spend their time today. He would also have had different travel options and somewhat different school subjects than students have today. He might have had a private tutor, or he might have begun working at age 12 and never attended school at all. This chapter addresses how historians identify and interpret the elements that make up the framework of a given time period in a given place. They examine people's ideas about life and what they valued and what they were concerned about. Historians pay attention to an event's geographical influences and to social and cultural issues of the day.

Historians are especially interested in capturing and explaining the significance of historical events. They want to understand how the issues involved in an event have developed over time and how an event has influenced people and other events across the years to the present time.

## DEVELOPING A HISTORICAL FRAMEWORK

According to Dr. James S. Olson, chairman of the history department at Sam Houston State University in Huntsville, TX, and author of 40 books about United States and World History, a good historian absolutely has to pay attention to historical frameworks and historical significance when researching a topic because every event in history must be looked at through its particular context. Olson says that establishing a historical framework helps a researcher see people as they lived in their own time and place and reminds students that they cannot judge people based on today's ideas and value systems (J. Olson, personal communication, January 12, 2005).

Olson gives Davy Crockett as an illustration of examining a person within his own time. He said that some people today are very critical of this hero of the Battle of the Alamo because he owned slaves. These critics ask, "How could a slave owner fight for the freedom of Texans when he held people in bondage?" They accuse him of being a hypocrite. Olson answers this accusation by noting that "you can't take a value system of today and impose it on a guy who lived in 1836." The professor is not advocating slavery, but reminding

| IDEAS AND VALUES: The ways people involved in a particular historical event thought about life. | GEOGRAPHICAL INFLUENCES: The difference time and place made in a particular historical event. |
| SOCIAL ISSUES: The ways people involved in a particular historical event related to each other. | CULTURAL ISSUES: The ways customs and traditions of people influenced the developments of a particular historical event. |

**Figure 5.** Elements of a historical framework: A window to the past.

*Note.* Give this tool to students to help them see an explanation of the four elements students must include as they engage in the CATCH process.

people who engage in historical research to avoid imposing current ways of thinking and being on people of the past. When developing a project, Olson advises students to read widely about the attitudes, values, and ideas of people who lived during this time and in this place.

How will students recognize the elements of historical framework as they research their topics? Four key elements make up a historical framework (see Figure 5). The first element examines *ideas and values* of people involved in an event. This area focuses on the way people looked at life in a given period of time. It reflects their values and their concerns. As students read about a particular time period, it is important for them to notice how people talked to each other. For example, did the people value manners? What were the concerns of the day and of the place? What did people think about their environment, the economy, human rights, the role of government in people's lives, or any other matters concerning a topic? As students investigate the people of a specific time period, they should try to capture what people cared about and how they went about attaining their goals. Imagine how radical it was for Victoria Woodhull to run for President of the United States against Ulysses S. Grant in 1872. At that time, women could not vote, serve on juries, or testify in court, yet she campaigned for the highest office in the United States. For this act, many people despised her, including some of the women suffragettes who were striving to gain the right to vote (Krull, 2004).

The second key element is *geographical influences*. Establishing the time and place of a historical event is important. Where people lived and the territory they were concerned about makes a great difference in students' understanding of the people who lived during a specific time period. How did the environment help or hinder them in their attempts to make a living? Were they isolated and wanted to establish contact with a larger part of the world? Were they often subjected to devastating storms and needed to rebuild their community? Did they need to establish warning systems against the dangers of the sea or of invading armies? For example, by looking at the physical setting of the American West, we see that life was quite different for the Sioux Indians before and after the Lewis and Clark Expedition because the coming of the White man drastically changed the environment of the West.

The third element concerns *social issues*. People either can be limited or benefited by their relationship to others and/or by the status of their position in life. Former President Jimmy Carter talked about growing up during the 1930s and 1940s on a farm in Georgia where his playmates were African American children. When they were very young, they regarded each other equally, but as they became teenagers, barriers slowly altered their friendship. They went to separate schools, could not sit together at a movie theater or even use the same drinking fountain. Eventually his African American friends started being polite to him in a way that elevated Jimmy Carter above them, and he knew that their closeness was dissolving due to racial distinctions. As a result, he felt a sense of loss by being part of a society that fostered a separation of races (Ifill, 2001). Examples of other social factors that have deeply affected individuals and groups across time include people's age, economic status, sex, and position in a community.

The final element of a historical framework is about *cultural issues*. Customs and traditions play a large role in the lives of people during a given time period. In some cultures, it is disrespectful for women to hold certain professional jobs, and men are expected to work in the same professions as their fathers. People's religious beliefs and practices also influence their actions. For example, these beliefs can influence how people vote and even what they buy so that both the government and the economy are sometimes shaped by people's religious ideas. Religious circumstances have even started new countries and settlements. In 1682, William Penn founded Pennsylvania to create a safe colony for Quakers, a sect of Christianity that firmly believed in peace and nonviolence. Quakers were severely persecuted in England, and William Penn even spent time as a prisoner in the Tower of London (Davison, 1993). Cultural issues often govern people's lives and therefore have played a large role in the development of historical events.

As students reflect on these elements of a historical framework, help them notice how interrelated they are. Consider how the circumstance of Jimmy Carter embodies all four of these elements in the following paragraph:

In the Deep South during the early to middle 20th century (geographical influence), people thought that White Americans were superior to African Americans (ideas and values). As they grew older, Jimmy Carter and his African American friends observed that African Americans were expected to show a certain respect to White Americans (social issues). Being separated in school and other public places reinforced this outlook (cultural issues).

## CAPTURING HISTORICAL SIGNIFICANCE

Historical significance can only be judged over large periods of time. Olson says that one way to measure a degree of relevance of this kind of impact is to see how an idea that was once unusual is now familiar and part of the mainstream. As an example, he refers to the concept of equality as Thomas Jefferson stated it in the *Declaration of Independence*:

When Thomas Jefferson wrote in that document that all men are created equal, nobody really believed him. Very few people believed in that principle. Today, in our society at least, you would have a hard time finding anybody who would disagree with that notion. (J. Olson, personal communication, January 12, 2005)

In this example, the idea of equality for all people has a high degree of historical impact because, over time, people have accepted it as part of our general way of thinking.

Another indicator of an idea's significance is that it remains a matter of discussion and debate over time. For example, according to Olson, isolationism in American foreign policy has been a point of debate since George Washington's presidency. During his administration, on June 5, 1794, Congress passed the Neutrality Act prohibiting Americans from participating in the military activities of a country other than the United States ("George Washington 1789–1797," n. d.). This act firmly established the United States as a neutral nation during conflicts between foreign countries, and at that time, the policy of isolationism was entrenched. However, as world circumstances changed, the stance of neutrality became a major issue again and again so that throughout

## Checklist for Measuring an Event's Historical Significance

|  | Yes | No |
|---|---|---|
| Does the event contain an unusual idea that has become part of mainstream thinking? | ❏ | ❏ |
| Does the event address an issue that remains a subject of discussion over time? | ❏ | ❏ |
| Does the event continue to influence our lives today? | ❏ | ❏ |

**Figure 6.** Checklist for determining historical significance.

our country's history, the level of America's involvement in the affairs of other nations has remained an issue of debate.

Olson says that there are four basic issues in American history that we turn to again and again. These issues include isolationism in American foreign policy, the role of the federal government in American life, civil rights in a multicultural society, and the relationship between people and their environment and between people and the land.

There are many ways to determine the historical significance of an event. Olson has presented three of them for students to consider: (a) an idea can be significant if it was once unusual, but over time it has become an accepted way of thinking; (b) a concept can be significant if people continue to make it an issue of discussion over time; and (c) an event is significant if it continues to influence our lives today. The questions provided in Figure 6 should help your students determine whether or not their topic has historical significance.

## APPROACHING A PROJECT LIKE A HISTORIAN

In order to create a project in the manner of a historian, students will want to pay special attention to components such as historical accuracy of events, people, issues, and structures; inclusive presentation of a subject's historical framework; and clear presentation of a subject's historical significance.

Students can capture these components through the CATCH process. Writing a paper is a choice vehicle for delving into the full historical framework and significance of an event. Creating a visual project reinforces the concepts a historical paper establishes. In some instances, students might create a project that illustrates only a segment of their paper. For example, if the subject of a project is about the construction of the Taj Mahal located near Agra, India, students might create the structure as a visual project. But, to discuss the model on an in-depth level with visitors at the display, students would need to understand the historical framework and historical significance of this amazing building. Writing a historical paper would equip students with this understanding.

In a historical paper, students could present the historical framework of India's character as it was in the 1600s, and explain how a ruler like Shah Jaban could live in splendor and grandeur and could afford to build such an elaborate burial place as the Taj Mahal for his beloved wife. Quoting the emperor, the paper would be able to show how even the speech of the day was as elaborate as the tomb he designed and constructed. As chief architect of the structure, he described his work as follows: "The sight of this mansion creates sorrowing sighs and makes the sun and moon shed tears from their eyes. In this world this edifice has been made to display thereby the Creator's glory" ("Taj Mahal Impressions," n. d.). The historical paper would also emphasize the historical significance of the Taj Mahal over the centuries.

By writing a historical paper, students become thoroughly familiar with their topic. Like a historian, they will be able to share their knowledge and understanding with authenticity.

As students work through creating their history fair projects, help them keep the elements of a historical framework and historical significance continually in mind. Thinking like a historian will guide them toward becoming a successful historian.

For students to practice identifying the elements of an event's historical framework and significance, you might choose to have them take the quiz included as Student Worksheet 1 in Appendix A (see p. 141), the student worksheets section. Answers for the quiz are included in the answer key in Appendix B (see p. 151). Another activity featured in Appendix A is an account of the story of Joan of Arc (Student Worksheet 2, see pp. 142–144). Students can apply their understanding of historical framework and historical significance by following the instructions accompanying the Joan of Arc story.

# CHAPTER 3

# Getting Started

Setting up and following an organizational plan at the beginning of a CATCH project will smooth the way for the work ahead. Making good decisions about certain components of a project is also a necessary step toward a good beginning. This chapter addresses both organizational and decision-making matters.

## Helping Students Organize Their Work

In designing a project, students will find setting up a schedule, using a checklist, and keeping a journal to be useful organizational tools as they assemble their thoughts and materials.

Setting up a schedule culminates with the due date you set for completing the historical paper and the visual project. It is wise for students to regulate their time to avoid trying to pull their project together at the last minute. For a suggested 6-week time frame, see Figure 7. This figure is just an example of a schedule. You might prefer to create your own for students to use as a reference as they progress in their work.

Using a checklist will help students reflect on their work so that they can be certain they are including all of the elements needed when writing a paper and constructing a project. Figure 8 offers a suggested checklist for students to use. As students complete each item, they should reflect on the extent to which they have fulfilled each task. For a quality product, they will want to represent each task to the best of their ability.

# Schedule for Developing a Historical Paper and Visual Project

**Week 1:**
- ❏ Explore possible topics.
- ❏ Decide on a topic.
- ❏ Read about the topic until a specific subject emerges that interests you.
- ❏ Read about the topic until an understanding of the topic's significance is apparent.
- ❏ Decide on a focus and formulate a guiding question to direct research.
- ❏ Make appointments for interviews.
- ❏ Set dates for trips to libraries and other places with sources of information.
- ❏ Begin research.

**Weeks 2 and 3:**
- ❏ Take careful notes of sources, using correct style for bibliographical entries.
- ❏ Begin work on annotated bibliography, indicating how each source is useful to understanding and communicating your topic.
- ❏ Develop ideas that answer guiding questions.
- ❏ Conduct interviews.

**Week 4:**
- ❏ Develop a premise statement.
- ❏ Decide which sources to use and how to use them to support your topic sentence.
- ❏ Reflect on the points that emerge from sources and conduct further research if necessary.
- ❏ Write the historic paper.
- ❏ Reflect on the writing and revise the work.

**Weeks 5 and 6:**
- ❏ Divide tasks for project construction among group members if working in a group.
- ❏ Assemble needed materials and equipment.
- ❏ Begin construction of the project.
- ❏ Continually reflect on the progress of the project.
- ❏ Complete construction of the project.
- ❏ Refine or revise your work.
- ❏ If entering a contest, develop questions you may be asked and practice answers to those questions.

**Figure 7.** Suggested schedule for developing a historical paper and visual project.

*Note.* This schedule is designed to help you and your students organize participation in CATCH. The schedule is based on a 6-week time frame. If you work from a shorter or longer time frame, you might want to use this schedule as an indicator of how students need to sequence their activities.

# Historical Project Checklist

## Historical Quality

- ❏ My work is historically accurate.
- ❏ My paper and project reflect a consistent historical framework that includes:
    - ❏ Ideas and values of the time period
    - ❏ Geographical influences
    - ❏ Social issues
    - ❏ Cultural issues
- ❏ My work clearly demonstrates my topic's historical significance.

## Research Quality

- ❏ My work shows a wide range of research.
- ❏ I have used _____ relevant primary sources.
- ❏ I have used _____ relevant secondary sources.
- ❏ My secondary and primary sources work together in support of each other.
- ❏ My research is balanced by the following:
    - ❏ Points of view
    - ❏ Types of materials

## Historical Paper

- ❏ I have stated a premise that requires interpretation using documentary evidence.
- ❏ My documentary evidence directly supports my premise.
- ❏ My conclusion summarizes and emphasizes my premise.

## Clarity of Presentation

- ❏ My written material is clear, organized, and appropriate.
- ❏ I have used correct and appropriate grammar.
- ❏ My visual project clearly represents my topic.

## Rules Compliance

- ❏ My product follows the guidelines my teacher has given to me.
- ❏ My bibliography follows the correct style.
- ❏ My bibliography is appropriately annotated.

**Figure 8.** Historical project checklist.

Conduct a class discussion to assist students in examining the elements on their checklist. Show how they match the points made during the discussion of historical research and writing in Chapter 2. In that chapter, Dr. Olson emphasized the importance of capturing the historical framework of events and the

## Instructions for Setting up Your Journal

1. Secure a one inch or one and a half inch three-ring binder with pockets inside the front and back covers.
2. Place the document "Schedule for Developing a Historical Paper and Visual Project" in the front binder pocket.
3. Place the document "Historical Project Checklist" in the back binder pocket.
4. Make a title page (either of your creation or by completing a form your teacher provides for you to complete). Include your name, the due date for the project and paper, the title of your historical paper, the title of your project, and the type of project you are completing.
5. Secure a package of five-tab pocket dividers. Dividers with pockets allow you to keep brochures and other materials you might pick up during the course of the project's development.
6. Place a few sheets of notebook paper behind each divider.
7. Label the divider tabs as follows:
   - Notations
   - To Do List
   - Context
   - Sources
   - Contacts

**Figure 9.** Instructions for setting up a journal.

people who lived during the times of an event. He also stressed how historians provide the historical significance of the topics and people they write about. To achieve historical quality, historians must engage in quality research methods as presented in Chapter 2. A detailed description and explanation of each element on this checklist will appear in future chapters. Students should be able to use this checklist to help direct them to create their best work.

Keeping a journal is an excellent way for students to organize their work. Figure 9 outlines how students should set up their journals and Figure 10 illustrates how the journal should look in a notebook.

One journal is sufficient for a group project. Students can pass the journal around as needed or they can write on loose-leaf notebook paper and add it to the journal. Encourage students to consult their schedule frequently, to mark completed items on their checklist as soon as they are completed, and to keep up with their journals in order to considerably facilitate their tasks.

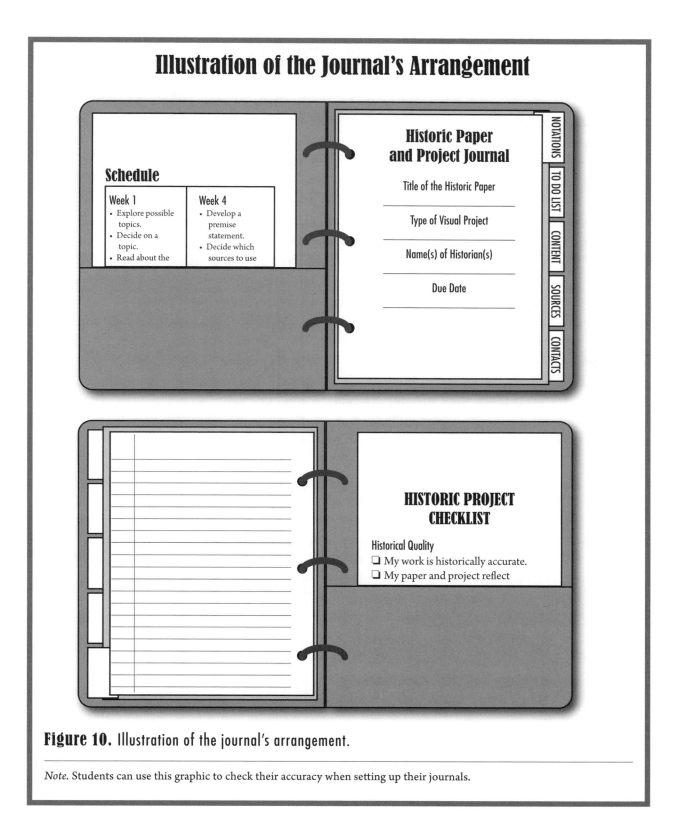

**Figure 10.** Illustration of the journal's arrangement.

*Note.* Students can use this graphic to check their accuracy when setting up their journals.

# Making Important Decisions

You and your students will have several decisions to make when you become involved in the CATCH process. Some of your decisions will depend on the nature of the history fair or festival that will display your students' projects. Other decisions are associated with factors such as students' abilities and interests, as well as the amount of time and resources available.

One decision-making consideration is whether to make your history fair competitive. You might want to give students the option of competing in a contest or of simply completing a class assignment. If you give students an option, you might need to help them decide which course of action is best for them to take. Whatever the choice students make, it is to the students' benefit to require everyone to follow the same standards for the project whether they enter a contest or not.

Another decision to make is if you want students to work alone or in groups. Sharing the workload in a major project can be quite an advantage, but some students might have an idea that they would like to pursue on their own. If your students are amenable, it would be good to give students a choice of working alone or in a group. Depending on the makeup of your class, you might want to decide whether to group your students ahead of time or allow them to group themselves.

Perhaps the most important decision about CATCH is your selection of the category of visual projects your students will construct, because these projects will need to capture the heart of your students' historical papers. Due to limited space availability for public displays, limited resources, or limited time, you might need to reduce these categories to a few choices for the students to make. Some teachers have their students create only one kind of visual project such as a model or a poster. Other teachers allow students to choose any of these categories:

- exhibits, scrapbooks, and posters;
- models and dioramas;
- performances (including plays, monologues, demonstrations, storytelling, reenactments, speeches, and simulations of historical trials); and
- media presentations (including videos, DVDs, computer presentations, and Web sites).

A brief description of each of these categories is outlined below. Detailed explanations, exact examples, and tools for constructing the projects appear in Chapter 6.

## EXHIBITS, SCRAPBOOKS, AND POSTERS

To construct an exhibit, students need to be able to communicate information succinctly by using few words and a pleasing design. Students with a talent for visually expressing what they have learned would enjoy using shapes, colors, and images to explain their topics. Students can also use media devices to enhance their exhibits.

Scrapbooks resemble a mini-exhibit. The pages of a scrapbook can tell a story about people involved in an event. Using their imaginations, students can pretend to be a person who kept a scrapbook while living through a battle-torn region, serving in a Roman household, or exploring the Congo River. Labels and brief pieces of text supplement collections of images and documents to bring to life the people who experienced a historical period.

Students who are judicious about the items they select to display can communicate a topic effectively by creating a poster. Posters appeal to students who have an artistic sense of composition and a succinct style of presentation.

## MODELS AND DIORAMAS

A model is a structure built to scale that accurately depicts a real structure. Students often enjoy constructing models of historically significant places such as forts, castles, and ships, and dwellings such as tents, sod houses, and plantation homes. Dioramas include models, but they are usually representative of large areas such as battlefields, village greens, and historical campsites.

## PERFORMANCES

Demonstrations are hands-on displays to help viewers understand how people of the past lived. In this category, students make objects from authentic materials and in the same manner historical people made them. Some examples include dipping candles, making dolls from cornhusks or fabric scraps, churning butter, making nautical knots, and grinding corn. Students might also demonstrate how people used certain objects such as stone scrapers, buttonhooks, stereopticons, and phonographs.

Explaining items from trunk exhibits are also interesting demonstrations. Students can give audiences an opportunity to guess the identity and use of historical objects and then explain what they are and how people used them. Usually trunk exhibits have a theme such as cowboy gear, pioneer household implements, farm tools, clothing from a certain era, or military gear.

A play or monologue is an effective way to communicate students' understanding of a significant event. The advantage of this activity is the opportunity to put oneself in the place of a person in the past so that the times of the event become real to both the dramatist and an audience. Writing and producing a drama requires deep research and a true understanding of the people students portray.

Storytelling sometimes can come from a real historical person's diary or similar account about an event. It can also be the telling of a story from the literature of a given culture. As a storyteller, a student will be able to reflect the emotions and attitudes of the people who experienced an event or who were part of a certain culture.

Reenactments are realistic reproductions of a significant historical event. As reenactors, students take on the roles of real people who experienced events in history through the centuries.

Speeches have been a significant part of history since the beginning of humankind. Often speeches about historical issues are persuasive. If students choose this kind of speech, they will be striving to convince an audience to take a certain course of action. For example, a student might try to convince a reluctant group of people to go to war or to add a certain amendment to the United States Constitution. Informative speeches also have had a place in historical events. Students might inform an audience of a certain circumstance such as the Holocaust or the roots of democracy found in ancient civilizations. These kinds of speeches are student created, not a recitation of a speech given by a historical figure, as a student might do in a reenactment. For example, delivering the Gettysburg Address would be a reenactment. Giving a talk informing an audience about the events surrounding the Battle of Gettysburg would be considered an original speech.

Presenting simulations of historical trials is a fascinating method for introducing historical controversies. Students act out what might have happened if a historical figure had actually been tried for a certain crime. For example, students might put Adolf Hitler on trial for genocide. Such a trial never took place, but students can gather evidence, develop witness testimony, and plan prosecutorial and defense strategies to write a script for a simulation of such a trial. The majority of the time, students take their scripts to a higher level, by acting in and conducting a mock trial based on what they've learned.

## MEDIA PRESENTATIONS

Video and DVD presentations usually center on historical sites and modern people discussing events related to the sites. For example, your school might be located near a battle site. Students could film that site, pointing out the places where significant events occurred on the battlefield. In order to explain the site's significance, students could film interviews with experts who

**Figure 11.** Artifacts from World War II era.

are familiar with the site, such as a curator of a museum or a professor at a university. Students could also include interviews with descendants of people who fought in the battle or witnessed the battle from a certain vantage point.

Computer presentations also center on historical events and historical figures. To construct this kind of presentation, students use pictorial documents, as well as taped interviews with knowledgeable people. Music and sound effects often enhance students' presentations.

Creating a Web site can be especially challenging for students and useful for people to access after its completion. In constructing a site, students would be able to include text, images, and links to other sites to inform others about a certain historical topic.

These are some of the visual projects you might consider to be appropriate for your students to create for display at a history event such as a fair or festival. Often, an audience will view the projects in stations. For example, the exhibits might be clustered together in one area, and computer presentations might be in a separate place. But, sometimes it is advantageous to combine certain projects on similar topics.

For example, students might demonstrate how people on the home front used certain artifacts from World War II. Another group could follow the demonstration with a play using the artifacts as props. Figures 11 and 12 present an example of this combination of visual projects. Figure 11 includes photos of several real-life artifacts from World War II. Figure 12 is a scene from a play called "The Pelfreys Pitch In," which uses several of the artifacts shown

# The Pelfreys Pitch In

## BY HELEN BASS

*JOEY:* Hey, look! The new issue of *Life* Magazine came today! (Picks it up from the table) Wonder if any new cars have come out.

*MARTHA:* (Entering) Say, Joey, have you heard that there's a war on? If you had picked up the string for that victory project you have going at school, you would know that. They are cutting back on car production, not making new ones.

*JOEY:* I know that! All the metal has to go for planes and tanks.

*MARTHA:* (Wistfully) Yeah, and ships like the ones Mama helps make at the Navy yard and the ship that Daddy is stationed on.

*JOEY:* (Quietly) Yeah. Hey, would you look at this: Chevrolet's ad. It's not about cars at all. Doesn't even show a car. It's about a conservation plan—conserve tires, conserve gas, conserve oil, on and on. Everything's about the war. I'm sick of it.

*MARTHA:* I know, Joey. So am I. Look at this old washboard. It says, "Victory Glass. Use this washboard made of materials not needed for defense and help win the war." And, oh my goodness, look at that ad. Even Kleenex tells you how you can be patriotic.

*JOEY:* Yeah, listen to this, "When sending the boys homemade cookies, fill crevices of the box with Kleenex. Prevents jiggling and breaking!" Gee whiz . . .

*MARTHA:* Look out the window, Joey. Here comes Mama. Oh, I have to get the washing off the table so we can have dinner. (Quickly removes the washtub and washboard)

*JOEY:* You might forget about that. She's not carrying any groceries.

*MARTHA:* But, she took all of our ration books with her today. She must have had enough stamps for something. She looks awfully tired. Maybe she just couldn't drag herself to the store.

*JOEY:* She always looks tired. That's because she does a man's job with the war on. I call her Rosie the Riveter, behind her back, of course.

**Figure 12.** Scene from "The Pelfreys Pitch In."

*Note.* This scene shows how students can use artifacts like those in Figure 11 to demonstrate everyday life during a historical time period; in this case, World War II. Adapted with permission from the Texas Education Agency. Copyright © Texas Education Agency. All rights reserved.

in Figure 11 to demonstrate a historically accurate home during World War II. A complete copy of the script for "The Pelfreys Pitch In" can be found in Appendix C (see p. 156).

Whatever you decide is best for your students as they engage in CATCH, it is important to help students create visual projects that tap their interests and talents and appropriately reflect the historical framework and historical significance presented in their papers. It also is important to help students keep focused and to use organizational tools that help them stay on track as they progress in writing their historical papers and constructing their visual projects.

# CHAPTER 4

# Researching Historical Papers

**Y**our students possibly have a topic for their historical papers in mind, but their ideas about their subject matter will not be fully developed until they have done fairly extensive research. It will be important for you to help students understand that the pattern for researching is often a back-and-forth process. Students begin with an interesting idea, and then they research it to find out more about it. As they discover new information, their ideas about their topics change, and so they return to sorting out how they want to approach their topics. Then, as part of the process, students formulate new ideas and discover that they need to do more research. This exploration phase of a project continues until students have their concept firmly in mind.

Students will likely continue this pattern of exploring, revising, and refining ideas until their work is complete. Even though this approach might appear to be haphazard, researching and writing actually follows an organized process that will be discussed in detail in the next two chapters. For an overview of the process, you might want to give students a copy of the graphic in Figure 13.

## The Exploration Phase

For best results in researching and writing a historical paper, students should follow a process. The first step is for students to explore their interests. In this phase, students read generally about a topic, searching for a focus they can use in their historical paper. A student might already know that she wants to make a model of a certain medieval castle, but in writing about this subject, she will eventually need to settle on a definite idea that presents the true

## The Research and Writing Process

**EXPLORE YOUR INTERESTS**

Read generally about a topic, searching for a focus for your historical paper.

**NARROW YOUR TOPIC**

Decide on a specific area of study.

**DEVELOP A PREMISE**

Identify the main points you want to make about your subject.

**FORMULATE GUIDING QUESTIONS**

Use them to direct your research.

**RESEARCH YOUR SUBJECT**

Collect data that supports your premise.

**WRITE YOUR PAPER**

State your premise in your introduction. Develop points that support your premise. Summarize with a strong conclusion.

**Figure 13.** The research and writing process.

historical significance of the castle and the historical framework for events that took place on the castle grounds.

During this phase, students need to find a topic they deeply enjoy, one that can absorb them. A historian must read in-depth about a topic before beginning to write about it. Students cannot understand their topic's historical framework and historical significance until they have explored it deeply. Because students will be spending a great amount of time on their topics, it is important for the topic to be of high interest to them.

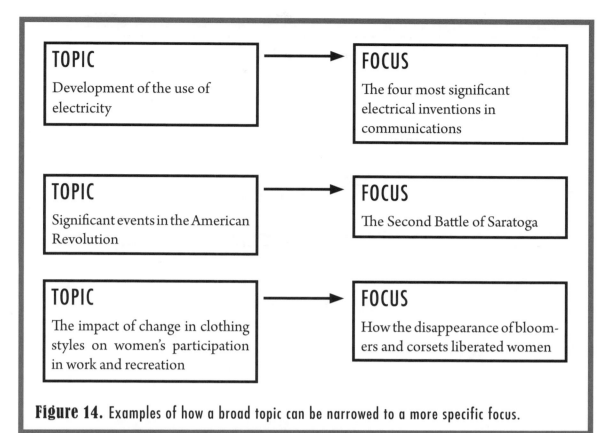

**Figure 14.** Examples of how a broad topic can be narrowed to a more specific focus.

# Narrowing the Topic

The next step is narrowing the topic to a focus. Getting acquainted with a topic through a source that gives an overview, such as a children's book, is a helpful way to begin research. As students look broadly at their topics, they will begin to establish a focus of concentration. Progress in developing a focus might look like one of the illustrations in Figure 14.

Topics are broad ideas within an even larger theme. In the narrowing process, students select a topic within a theme. The topic narrows to a focus. The focus then narrows to specific subject matter. The narrowest piece, the title, will reflect the focus of the topic.

For example, you might want your class to write historic papers that depict the broad theme of the American Civil War era, including events that led up to the conflict. One appropriate choice for a topic would be the Missouri Compromise passed by the United States Congress in 1820. At that time, the nation was regularly adding new states to the Union. A major issue was whether the new states would allow slavery. The Missouri Compromise declared that Missouri would enter the Union as a slave state, but any new states located north of Missouri would come in as free states. This meant that Missouri could allow slavery, but certain states entering the Union after 1820 could not.

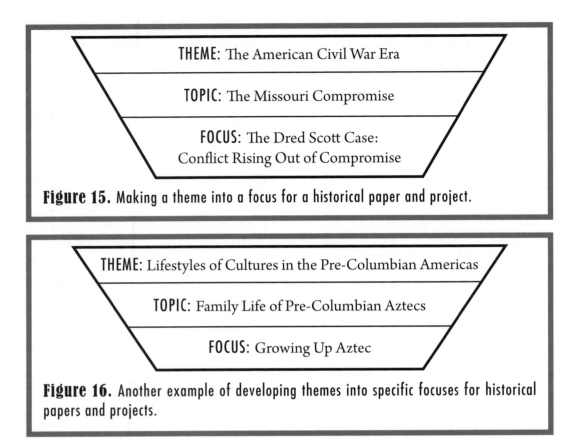

**Figure 15.** Making a theme into a focus for a historical paper and project.

**Figure 16.** Another example of developing themes into specific focuses for historical papers and projects.

As a topic, the Missouri Compromise is still a broad subject, so the title, representing the focus, would need to indicate how the student was going to address only one result of that compromise. The Dred Scott case would be a fitting focus to show how the Missouri Compromise became a factor leading up to the Civil War (see Figure 15). Dred Scott was a slave who had served his master in both slave and free states as his master moved from place to place. After the master died, a lawyer helped Dred Scott sue for freedom because although he had lived in Missouri, a slave state, he had also lived in Wisconsin, a state that had entered the Union as a free state under the Missouri Compromise. The case went all the way to the United States Supreme Court, and the Court ruled that Dred Scott should remain a slave. The decision greatly angered people in the United States who were against slavery, and many historians believe that the outcome of the case was one of the major causes of the Civil War (Davis, 1990).

Consider another example. Perhaps the theme for your students' project is "Lifestyles of Cultures in the Pre-Columbian Americas." This is a broad concept that covers all cultures in North and South America, so it would be necessary to narrow the theme to a topic. Family life of Pre-Columbian Aztecs would be an appropriate topic, but a student writing about this topic would need to narrow the idea to a specific focus (see Figure 16).

Selecting a specific area such as what it would be like to grow up as an Aztec would indicate that the project centers on Aztec children. This would be a suitable area of concentration because the Aztecs had many rituals involving the birth, naming, and raising of children. For example, education and training was a very serious matter for these people who ruled the area of land that is today Mexico City. Parents of both noble and working class societies had high expectations of their children and firmly directed them in achieving definite goals. Each child attended a school, one for upper-class students and one for lower-class children. Boys and girls went to separate schools and because girls were always chaperoned, they were forbidden to talk to boys if they happened to pass one another. At the school, boys were subjected to harsh practices so that they could be toughened for warfare. One requirement for boys was to regularly draw blood from their ears and legs. Girls went to boarding schools and were awakened several times a night to offer incense to their gods and pray (Bray, 1958).The subject of growing up Aztec would be quite enlightening for students to study within the broader theme of "Lifestyles of Cultures in the Pre-Columbian Americas."

As students narrow their topics to a central focus, they will be able to identify the historical significance of their event. For example, narrowing the Civil War theme to the Dred Scott case helps students understand how the issues of sectionalism directly affected individuals of the period and how the Dred Scott decision fueled the march toward war. This micro look gives meaning to the macro condition of the United States during the antebellum era. Identifying the significance of their topic will prepare students to begin the next phase of their research: developing a premise.

# Developing a Premise

A premise is an assertion that requires evidence for a conclusion. Sometimes a premise is stated as an issue. Other times a premise is an opinion about the impact of an event over time. Using a premise gives students a base for all they demonstrate about a topic, and it generates the historical significance of that topic. For example, consider a premise statement asserting that the implements, personal items, and botanical and zoological life early English colonists brought to Jamestown drastically and forever altered the area's environment (Lange, 2007). The statement provides a base for students to build on because it shows the evidence students need to gather to address the assertion that these particular factors contributed to environmental change. The statement generates historical significance because it provides students a starting point toward developing a case for these factors making a strong impact over time. A premise also allows historians to interpret events rather than simply collect facts or anecdotes and elaborate on them. A focus and a premise work together to articulate the "so what?" or significance of a topic.

It might be beneficial to your students to complete the activities in Worksheets 3 (Characteristics of a Premise; see p. 145) and 4 (Is It a Premise?; see p. 146) in Appendix A at the end of this book. In these activities, students examine premise and nonpremise statements and then identify three characteristics of premises.

An example of a premise statement is: The decision to use the atomic bomb had the greatest impact of any decision the American government made during the 20th century. This is a premise statement because its assertion about the level of impact of the decision to use the atomic bomb requires supporting evidence and interpretation. It also sets the stage for presenting a conclusion, and it lays a foundation for the topic's significance.

An example of a nonpremise statement on this subject is: The United States dropped atomic bombs on two Japanese cities during World War II. This is a nonpremise statement because it simply states a fact that is easily corroborated. It does not require supporting evidence or interpretation.

Once students have their premises firmly in mind, they will be able to direct their research efforts in a constructive and meaningful manner, because a premise statement not only requires supporting evidence and a conclusion, but also gives direction to the scope of the topic. Armed with a premise, students will be ready to advance to the next step in the research and writing process: formulating guiding questions.

# Formulating Guiding Questions

Guiding questions emerge from a premise and help students decide which sources to examine and which sources to leave alone as they conduct their research. A guiding question is flexible and can be modified as students increase their database of information about a topic. The nature of these questions prevents them from having "yes" and "no" answers. Like premises, they require interpretation. Figure 17 provides examples of both workable and nonworkable guiding questions for certain topics.

Now, let's look at some sample premises and some workable guiding questions for each.

**Premise:** At a crucial time for American Forces in the Pacific, a group of Navajos developed and implemented the most significant military code used during World War II.

**Guiding Questions:** Why did this code succeed while others failed? How was this code different from other codes? Why and how were the Navajos who developed the code especially qualified for this assignment? How was the code implemented? What were the significant results of using the code?

**Premise:** The decision to use the atomic bomb had the greatest impact of any decision the American government made during the 20th century.

**Guiding Questions:** Why did the United States use such a drastic measure as the atomic bomb? What alternative action could the U.S. have taken? Why did the U.S. drop more than one atomic bomb? How did the U.S. decide which cities to bomb? How did dropping the bomb lead to ending the war? What was the exact impact of using this bomb and why was this so significant? What influence does this act have in today's warfare strategies?

**Premise:** Bob Hope played a significant role in boosting the morale of U.S. troops stationed in combat zones during World War II through his commitment to bringing entertaining shows and by assuring his audience that they were fighting to save the American way of life and values.

**Guiding Questions:** What was the evidence that the state of the morale of the American troops was low before Bob Hope arrived? What conditions affected the morale of the American troops? How did Bob Hope specifically address these conditions? How effective were Bob Hope's efforts? What were the significant results of Bob Hope's visit to American troops? How do people today regard Bob Hope's war efforts?

| Guiding Question (Invites an Interpretation) | Nonguiding Question (Requires Only a Limited Response) |
|---|---|
| Why is jazz considered to be America's most original art form? | What is considered to be America's most original art form? (Jazz would answer the question without further discussion.) |
| How did Mohandas Gandhi's peaceful approach to protest expedite India's attaining independence from Britain? | What were some of Mohandas Gandhi's peaceful approaches to protesting? (A descriptive list would serve as an answer.) |
| How did President Truman's personal beliefs influence the implementation of the Marshall Plan after World War II? | What were the accomplishments of the Marshall Plan? (A list would suffice as an answer.) |

**Figure 17.** Examples of workable and nonworkable guiding questions.

In formulating guiding questions, students might rely on newspaper reporters' stand-by prompts such as who, what, why, and how. Figure 18 provides a graphic example of how these prompts can be used to develop guiding questions. This graphic could be a useful reference source for students as they formulate their own guiding questions.

When students develop "who" questions, they should be sure to state their reasons for selecting a certain person and then support their reasons with data from their research. An example of a good "who" question is: *Who* was the most destructive, contributive, or significant person or group among Greek playwrights?

Answering "what" questions requires students to identify the significance of an event with supportive statements that demonstrate the impact of the event over time. An example of a good "what" question is: *What* was significant about the construction of the Great Wall of China?

Student answers to "why" questions require additional explanations and interpretations of causes for certain events. An example of a good "why" question is: *Why* did Great Britain send prisoners to Australia?

Answering "how" questions involves students interpreting the time period during which the event took place and examining the circumstances surrounding the event. An example of a good "how" question is: *How* did The Beatles change the music industry?

Formulating guiding questions at the beginning of students' research will enable them to keep their research focused and on target with their topic and premise.

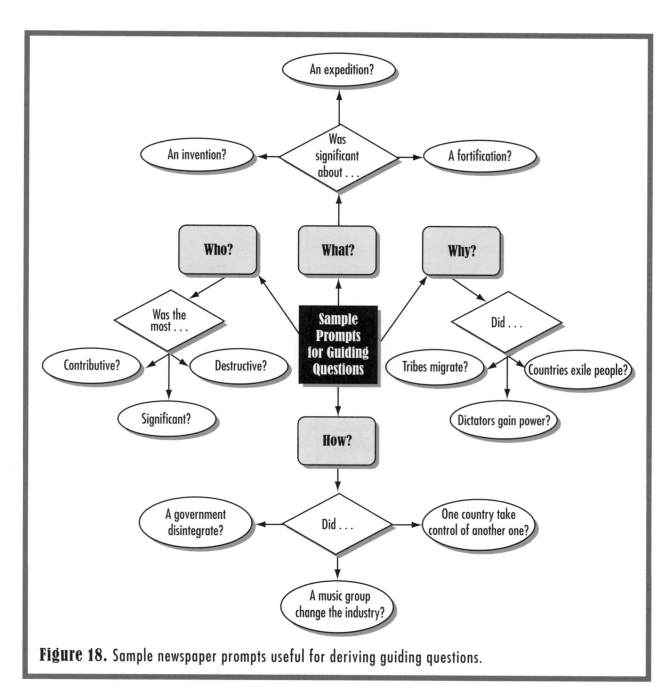

**Figure 18.** Sample newspaper prompts useful for deriving guiding questions.

# Gathering Data and Researching the Subject

Now that students have a focus, premise, and guiding questions, it is time for them to begin their research in earnest. The main consideration at this point is searching for sources yielding information that supports a premise and that informs students about the elements of the historical framework of their topics. For example, if students are looking for information about Bob Hope's efforts to build troop morale, they would find some of the following information that fits into the historical framework:

- *Ideas and values of the period*—Being involved in World War II was an absorbing circumstance for civilians and military personnel. Fear dominated all people at home, as well as those deep into combat zones. United States citizens were called on to dismiss all of their ambitions for the duration of the war. Military personnel had to fight rather than continue their education, pursue nonmilitary careers, or live a settled life with their families. Civilians dreaded getting the news that a loved one had been killed. People feared attacks by Japanese planes on America's West Coast like those that bombarded Pearl Harbor, and they feared invasion by Germans on the United States' eastern shores. They sacrificed common necessities for the war effort. Everyone had to adjust to the hardships of wartime. These conditions shaped peoples' values and attitudes. How did such conditions affect Bob Hope's programs of entertaining the troops? Through humor and entertainment, Bob Hope could make people laugh and offer at least a short amount of time for forgetting all that was assailing them. Loved ones at home were comforted that their troops were attending and enjoying performances by the same entertainers civilians listened to on the radio at home. In this way, Bob Hope offered a kind of connection between home and foreign fields ("Bob Hope and American Variety," 2004).

- *Geographical influences*—Danger threatened the cast and crew of Bob Hope's group every time they traveled to a war zone. Disease, fatigue, and enemy fire were factors of grave concern. Remoteness of entertainment sites was also a consideration for those who had the job of setting up stages and connecting microphones and amplifiers to sources of electricity. Describing the physical conditions of these tours would help establish the significance of Bob Hope's programs because doing so emphasizes the sacrifice each troupe member was making (Deaton, 2003).

- *Social issues*—Part of Bob Hope's humor was akin to comedians today who poke fun at politicians and others in public life. Even having the nerve to do this reminded the troops that they were fighting for essential American freedoms such as free speech. Bob Hope had to be sensitive to what he said, however. His mission was to boost morale, not discourage those who needed to be reminded that their sacrifices were appreciated, as well as necessary ("Letters from the GIs," n. d.).

- *Cultural issues*—Even the selection of songs the entertainers sang was important to the morale of the troops. This was a sentimental era because people were apart from those they loved for long periods of time. They felt loneliness and occasionally a deep heartache by this separation. Also, many of those fighting were trying to cope with the horrors they had experienced when under enemy attack. Sentimental songs could help soldiers connect with their feelings, but they could also stimulate depression. Bob Hope had to line up an evening of entertainment that would balance sentiment with comedy and just plain fun (Connaughton, 2001).

Including the elements of a historical framework is vital to the support of a historian's premise. Students need to consult a variety of sources to gain enough information to support a premise and to construct a quality and comprehensive historical paper.

As you make research and writing assignments, students will always ask many questions about source material. Below are some of the questions you might be called on to answer.

## HOW MANY SOURCES DOES A HISTORICAL PAPER NEED?

A specific number of sources is not required. As students engage in research they will begin to acquire a feel for exactly what kind of sources are needed to tell a full story, and they eventually will understand their topics well enough to know when they have finished their research. Sometimes you might ask students questions to help them decide if they need to do more research. For example, you might ask if they have enough information to give a good account of a certain element of the historical framework of a topic such as the influence of the geographical setting of an event. Stress to your students that for a thorough treatment of their topics, they will need to investigate both primary and secondary sources.

## WHAT ARE PRIMARY SOURCES?

A primary source is a document written or produced during a topic's time period that gives firsthand knowledge about an event. Examples of primary sources include letters, legal papers, speeches, diaries, newspapers, photographs, artwork, artifacts, and oral histories.

## WHAT DO PRIMARY SOURCES DO?

Primary sources bring people and events to life. They provide examples of how people felt, what they believed, how they expressed themselves, and what they valued. Primary sources authenticate a topic because they demonstrate real people experiencing real events. In this way they capture excitement, fear, sorrow, humiliation, joy, and other emotions someone felt during an event. Primary sources also help a researcher make a personal interpretation of an incident. Students should look at as many primary sources as possible, then compare and contrast what they can about their general significance, according to Dr. James Olson. Looking at primary sources also will help your students determine the kinds of secondary sources they need to examine. Examples of ways primary sources help a researcher gain a perspective of reality about an event include:

- *Artwork*—Native Americans, Aboriginals of Australia, and ancient people of Europe and Africa have left their stories painted and carved on rocks and in caves. Studying these representations and symbols in rock art helps an observer see what was important to the artist and can occasionally point to a approximate time period of the artwork. For example, a horse's appearance in Native American rock art places the time of the drawing after Columbus came to America because horses were not reintroduced to North America until Europeans brought these animals to the continent.

- *Documents*—Deeds, death certificates, wills, and census records provide exact information about people. For example, if a researcher wanted to determine if a specific person had owned a particular valuable heirloom, his last will and testament would be a good source of information because he probably would have passed the item on as an inheritance.

- *Photographs*—Battlefield photographs evoke feelings of horror and sorrow as they depict bodies strewn across the ground. Photographs also give researchers practical information about clothing and hairstyles of people in a given time and place. For example, a teenaged girl with bobbed hair in the 1920s was probably a very modern young lady.

- *Letters*—Written words in a person's own handwriting provide a definite reality for a researcher. Thomas Jefferson's letter to Meriwether Lewis about his mission to explore and report on the land west of the Missouri River after the Louisiana Purchase shows precisely what Americans wanted to know at that time about this strange and mysterious territory. President Jefferson made it clear that the expedition should obtain plant and animal specimens not found east of the Mississippi River. Other mandates in this letter help the researcher comprehend where the United States was in its understanding of western Native American tribes. The letter also reveals the high hopes of finding connecting waterways that would increase the trade advantages of the United States all the way to the Pacific Ocean ("Jefferson's Letter," n. d.). Reading this letter gives the researcher a sense of the impact the Lewis and Clark expedition made on the United States because of all the ways these western lands changed as a result of the expedition's reports in answer to Jefferson's letter.

- *Artifacts*—Viewing and handling an object used in another time period gives a researcher a strong sense of the people who lived in a given time and place. A British soldier's ordeal of fighting in the American heat and humidity becomes real when touching a woolen uniform and a furry mohair backpack that an actual Revolutionary War soldier was required to wear. Gazing at a beautiful set of china dishes a woman was forced to abandon to lighten the load of her wagon on the Oregon Trail brings a sense of loss and a reality of hardship to a researcher.

- *Diaries and journals*—People usually express their deep feelings and true reactions to events they have observed when writing in their diaries. These writings are valuable to a researcher trying to capture the impact of events. In Charleston, SC, Mary Chestnut watched the battle of Fort Sumter from her rooftop. Her diary tells of her fears for her husband and of the frantic screams of the other women huddled with her crying out at every cannon boom (Chestnut, 1861/1997).

- *Eyewitness accounts*—Interviews of people who were actually on the scene of an event are valuable for giving the human interest or emotional side of an event, as well as for giving personal impressions of what actually occurred. Listening to an adult tell about her suffering of being a young child with polio gives a researcher an understanding of how important it was for Jonas Salk and his colleagues to give the world a prevention of this dreaded disease. Also, people who have participated in protest marches or picket lines give the researcher a sense of the fervor of those who are willing to take risks for a cause. A collection of eyewitness accounts can help provide a balanced view of an event.

## WHAT ARE SECONDARY SOURCES?

A secondary source is a publication by an author who was not an eyewitness or a participant in an event. The author writes about events using primary sources and offers factual or interpreted accounts. Examples of secondary sources include textbooks, biographies, and encyclopedias.

## WHAT DO SECONDARY SOURCES DO?

Secondary sources provide information about people and events by interacting with primary sources. One of the ways these sources interact is that secondary sources interpret and explain primary sources. Sometimes a diary or letter only reveals a small portion of a bigger picture, so a researcher needs more information to understand why a document is important. Anne Frank's diary is touching and makes the terrors of the Holocaust real to those who read it. However, to fully appreciate Anne's account, the researcher also needs to know about the issues and events that explain why Anne and her family were hiding and why the discovery of her family was horribly devastating. Books and other secondary sources about the Holocaust describe what was happening in the rest of Europe during the time Anne wrote her diary and help the reader understand Anne's circumstances.

Another way the sources interact is that secondary sources demonstrate how primary sources fit into a topic's historical framework. Primary and secondary sources work together to tell the entire story about the people participating in a given event, about the influential geographical features of an area, and about the social and cultural influences that bear on a topic.

Finally, secondary sources show how primary sources contribute to an understanding of the topic's historical significance. An intimate acquaintance with Anne Frank's diary gives a researcher a deep understanding of how the Holocaust was devastating to one family, and sources written about the Holocaust help a researcher understand the powerful impact the Holocaust continues to have on the world today.

## HOW DOES A RESEARCHER DISTINGUISH BETWEEN A PRIMARY AND SECONDARY SOURCE?

Usually the distinction is obvious, but occasionally researchers uncover a source that is not completely clear. Students should ask the following question to determine if a source is primary: Does this source provide firsthand knowledge about a topic? For example, The Laramie Treaty, made in 1868, is a primary source. It declared that the land between the Missouri River and the Rocky Mountains would remain Indian Territory forever. A magazine article written in the 21st century about how the treaty was broken would be a secondary source even if it contained quotes from participants at the signing of the treaty. For a helpful discussion about primary and secondary sources, see the University of California at Berkeley Library Web site (http://www.lib.berkeley.edu/TeachingLib/Guides/PrimarySources.html).

## HOW DO RESEARCHERS FIND THE PRIMARY AND SECONDARY SOURCES THEY NEED?

The first step in research is gaining an overview of the topic. Kansas history teacher Chris Terrill suggests beginning with a children's book, because such a source will explain the basic elements of the events in question. Textbooks are also helpful because they not only cover the basics of a topic, but also include a bibliography that provides the sources the authors used in writing the book. Some textbooks include primary accounts of events and supplementary materials that include a list of primary sources.

Next, visits to the school library and a local public library will uncover more resources, and those sources will provide reference to even more sources. University libraries offer further support.

Museums display useful artifacts and information, and often their gift shops sell books and documents that are difficult to find in other markets. Museum personnel are knowledgeable and can help with suggestions about places to find available sources.

Occasionally, an author of a resourceful book will be willing to give a researcher an interview. Book jackets sometimes tell the city and state of an author's residence, or you can send a letter to an author in care of the publisher. Many authors also have Web sites with an invitation to e-mail them.

The Internet is an excellent source of information because it carries information from researchers all over the world. When using this source, caution students that some of the articles might not be authentic or valid. It is safe to stay with Web sites for museums, official historical centers, university libraries, historical preservation organizations such as the Daughters of the American Revolution, and government educational resources. Simply typing in "primary sources" and the name of a topic into a search engine can also yield an abundance of Web sites.

## INTERVIEWS

As students research their topics, they will enjoy the experience of seeing their primary and secondary sources blend together to tell a complete story of a significant human experience. If they are writing about recent history, one of the best sources could be an interview with someone who experienced the event a topic concerns.

Listening to a person give an account of his or her participation in an event gives a researcher a strong sense of reality and a feel for a deep significance of what happened. Personal stories bring authenticity to episodes that have made a difference in people's lives. For example, people who lived through wars, the

## Table 2
## Useful Oral History Web Sites

**Oral History Society**
http://www.oralhistory.org.uk/advice

**Indiana Center for the Study of History and Memory, Oral History Techniques**
http://www.indiana.edu/~cshm/techniques.html#top

**Library of Congress, Techniques for Conducting Oral History Interviews**
http://memory.loc.gov/ammem/ndlpedu/lessons/oralhist/ohguide.html

**Rutgers' Oral History Archives**
http://oralhistory.rutgers.edu

**History Matters—Making Sense of Oral History**
http://historymatters.gmu.edu/mse/oral

**American Memory, Library of Congress**
http//lcweb2.loc.gov/ammem/

**Oral History Abstracts From the Institute of Texan Cultures**
http://www.texancultures.utsa.edu/memories/htms/abstracts.htm

Holocaust, natural disasters, the assassination of President Kennedy, immigration, founding an important local establishment, Native American relocations, or the Great Depression are excellent resources for capturing the effect these events had on individuals. The incidents they discuss may or may not be dramatic, but they are important for helping others understand what happened and how it felt to be part of the event.

How do students find people to interview? Perhaps they already have someone in mind. You, your students, or their parents may know people who have participated in an event that is related to a certain topic. Other sources that might be able to provide names of appropriate people to interview are local historical societies, genealogy groups, or service clubs. Helpful groups outside the community might include curators of museums, history professors, and directors of headquarters of historical places such as the Country Music Hall of Fame in Nashville, TN, or NASA's Johnson Space Center in Houston, TX. Certain Web sites are also helpful in finding subjects for and conducting oral history interviews. Table 2 provides some examples of such Web sites.

Students should avoid making a general appeal such as taking out newspaper ads or posting messages on bulletin boards because it is best to interview a reliable and truly authentic person who genuinely represents the topic of the historical paper. Students should secure a recommendation from a reputable organization or from a trusted individual.

If an oral history source is available locally, it is best to conduct an interview in a personal visit. However, if the person lives far away, it is appropriate to interview a person by telephone or e-mail. If long-distance interviews are in order, students should ask for permission to interview and once permission is secured, set up a time to conduct the interview. Whether an interview is local or long distance, students should always use procedures of etiquette and effective means of obtaining relevant information.

See Table 3 for a guide to conducting interviews. This guide provides students with procedures for conducting successful interviews.

## BALANCED RESEARCH

As students accumulate their primary and secondary sources, they need to make sure their collection is balanced. The term *balanced research* refers to two areas. The first part refers to using a variety of types of sources. For example, in a paper about a soldier's life in the jungles of Vietnam, it would certainly be important to cite and quote letters that he wrote and received during his tour of duty in the war. But, other documents such as Web sites, newspaper articles, political speeches, and books enlarge the scope of the situation and help tell the full story.

The second part of balanced research refers to point of view. Centering on one soldier's viewpoint is an effective way to deepen understanding of the circumstances, but an even greater understanding comes from examining viewpoints of those who supported the soldier, as well as the opinions of those who disagreed with him. What did the soldier's wife think about the news her husband wrote in his letters to her? What did his buddies think about what was happening? What did his commanding officers think about these circumstances? What were the thoughts of a Viet Cong soldier also fighting in the jungle? Did the soldier have the same or different ideas about the Vietnam War as protesters back home?

As students research their topics, they need to make deliberate efforts to balance their research in order to present a thorough treatment of their topics when they write their historical papers.

## BUILDING AND ANNOTATING A BIBLIOGRAPHY

How will students keep track of all of the information their sources yield? The most helpful way is to carefully note each source at the time a student consults it. Students might not use all of the documents they examine when they write a paper, but they can greatly help themselves if they are thoroughly

## Table 3
## A Guide to Conducting Successful Oral History Interviews

1. Get in touch with the person first by telephone if possible.

2. Always identify yourself to the person, supplying your name, your school's name, and the purpose of your project. Tell the person how you believe he or she could provide information that would help you with your topic.

3. When the person agrees to see you, set up a time for the interview. Remember to ask if you can use a tape recorder or video camera during the interview.

4. Formulate your questions so that they directly pertain to your topic and answer a portion of your guiding questions.

5. Provide your subject with a copy of the questions you plan to ask in plenty of time prior to the interview so he or she can read and think through the questions before the interview.

6. During the interview:

   • Be polite and respectful. Be aware that this person is giving you his or her time and might be nervous about discussing an incident or time period that could be personal and sensitive.

   • Put both yourself and your subject at ease by asking one or two basic questions about the person before you launch into those questions designed to bring out the depth of the person's experience. Examples of basic questions include: Have you lived here long? Where did you grow up? Do you have children? How did you come to live here? Often a person will elaborate on these questions, and talking about general topics will help the person relax. Remember not to take too much of the person's time, so move on to the questions you came to ask after you spend a few minutes in small talk.

   • Ask open-ended questions that require more than a yes, no, or one-word answer. For example: How did you become interested in being a chaplain? What did you think when you learned that you were going to be stationed in Vietnam? How did you feel being in enemy territory without a weapon?

   • Politely keep the person you are interviewing on track. Occasionally people wander into other topics without realizing they are doing so. One refocusing technique could be: "That's very interesting, and I'm also interested in how conducting religious services in a jungle was different than inside a church."

- Avoid asking sensitive or personal questions. An example of a sensitive question: "Can you describe a time when you didn't know how to answer a soldier's religious questions?" Instead say, "Please describe the most difficult part of being a chaplain of soldiers in frightening circumstances."

- Ask if the subject has anything else to add that would help you better understand the circumstances of the event. A person who has lived through an experience has insights that others do not know about.

- Ask the person if he or she knows another person who might have a story to tell that relates to your topic.

7. Write a thank you note to the person you interviewed.

8. Transcribe the tape recording right away while the interview is still fresh. If part of it is unclear, contact the subject for clarification.

acquainted with each piece they consult. It is helpful for students to record a brief summary of each source's content and to make a note of how that source is useful to writing about the topic.

As students make these notations, they will be accumulating information for an annotated bibliography. An annotated bibliography is not only useful to the writer, but it is a great help to those who read and judge a historical paper because this document offers one way for students to demonstrate their understanding of a topic. It also speaks of the variety of sources students consulted, and it reflects a student's efforts to present a balanced view of a topic. A guide to completing and writing an annotated bibliography is available in Table 4.

This part of the research process is important and requires a student's full attention. David Miller, a student who has created many history projects says, "The annotated bibliography is the hardest part of the project. You've got to put as much as you can into it. You can't just slap it together."

And, history teacher Chris Terrill advises her students to keep their annotated bibliographies as they go along, so as not to overwhelm themselves at the end of the research and writing process (personal communication, November 19, 2005).

Here is an example of an annotated entry of a primary source:

Reynolds, Kay. Personal Interview. 10 March 2006.

Mrs. Reynolds had polio when she was 3 years old and the horrors of her experience are still vivid for her today, 60 years later. As I listened to her story about her physical pain, paralysis, separation from her parents, being tied to bed, and the terror of watching a child in the bed next to her die, I understood how important it was to discover a cure for polio.

## Table 4
## A Guide to Compiling and Writing an Annotated Bibliography

1. When you prepare your bibliography, separate the listing of your primary and secondary sources.

2. Keep your language dignified. Avoid using slang and casual expressions that degrade your source.

3. Keep your annotation honest. Avoiding padding it with meaningless statements to make your bibliography look long and complicated. One to three sentences will suffice to convey how a source was a factor in your project.

4. Avoid plagiarism. This is the practice of implying that the work of another person is your own work. Always give credit to your sources and place direct quotes in quotation marks.

5. Tell how each source genuinely contributed to your project and to your understanding of a topic. Your paper will reflect the role the sources played in your presentation, so your claims about them will be obvious.

6. Remember to keep careful notes of every source. Avoid wasting time searching for a document that would be readily available if you had noted its location initially.

7. Exhaust your run of sources. Follow up when one source leads to another one. Let people know about your research. Someone could encounter a source while you are in the process of investigating your topic and direct you to it.

8. Do not think that you must use every source you find. Some references may give you a bit broader or deeper understanding of your topic, but you may not actually use them in your final product. If you did not use a source, you cannot legitimately cite it.

9. Always keep your premise and guiding questions in mind. Pay close attention to your true investigation. For example, consider the question: Why were wagon trains important to the development of the American West? In the course of researching this topic, you might discover how a few families occasionally separated from the train thinking they could follow a shortcut to Oregon. These people usually found themselves in serious trouble and their adventures provide fascinating reading, but their experiences have nothing to add to your historical paper. Do not allow yourself to become sidetracked.

Here is an example of annotating a secondary source:

Anthony, Aubrey Ray. *Eradicating Polio*. Boston: Seymour Riley and Sons Press, 1999.

**Table 5**
**Examples of Turabian Style in Bibliography Entries**

**Book: Single Author**

Author. *Book title*. Place of publication: Publisher, date.

Ellis, Joseph J. *His Excellency: George Washington*. New York: Random House, 2004.

**Article in a Magazine**

Author. "Article Title." *Magazine*, date, volume number.

Michaels, Alma Louise. "My Day With Jimmy and Rosalyn Carter." *Americans All*, 25 July 2001, 87.

This book tells how desperate people were to make the polio vaccine available to all school children as soon as possible. It helped me understand how the science and medical communities often work together to help rid the world of harmful diseases. It also explained how serious and widespread polio was in the mid-20th century.

Encourage students when they tend to succumb to the tedium of working on their bibliographies. Even though compiling and annotating a bibliography can be routine, it also can be an enjoyable experience. Finding just the right source and conducting successful interviews are exciting and rewarding accomplishments. Students will feel profound satisfaction when they see their final bibliography spread before them as a typed testimony of their persistent hard work.

An important part of constructing annotated bibliographies is using a correct universal standard of documentation or style guides. One of the most respected and often used style guides for historical papers is Kate L. Turabian's *A Manual for Writers of Term Papers, Theses, and Dissertations* (1996). Examples for the correct style for the most common citations are listed on the Web site "Turabian Style Guide" (http://www.libs.uga.edu/ref/turabian.html).

Your school library will probably have copies of these guides, and librarians are always ready to help students with bibliographical style. Table 5 also shows two common examples of Turabian citations that may be helpful.

Thoroughly researching a topic is vital in the process of writing a historical paper, so students need to build a strong bank of sources. Even after students have begun writing, ideas may occur to them that require further research.

Spending all of the time necessary to engage in research is a worthwhile endeavor because quality research will contribute to the quality of the final product. Uncovering data and following leads can be an exciting venture, so encourage your students to delve into the task with high expectations and an abundance of enthusiasm.

At this point, it is beneficial to return to the idea of students keeping a journal. Students received instructions for setting up a journal in Chapter 3, but the contents of the divisions were not provided because they contain terminology about the writing process that students had not encountered. After you have taught students about the process, you might want to discus the contents of their journal with them. Content information and tips about keeping each section of the journal are listed in Table 6.

Although students need to work from their own integrity, they will depend on you to guide them and help them stay on a focused track as they go through the writing process like a historian.

# Table 6
# Section Contents for Student Journal

The sections of your journal should include these contents:

1. *Notations*: This section is for jotting down your guiding questions, your premise, and relevant thoughts and impressions you will form as your project develops. For example, in the exploration phase of your project you might record possible topics and eventually possible titles. As you research, you could record the advantages and disadvantages of working with the topics and ideas you are considering. Some advantages could include an abundance of primary sources or your high interest in the subject. Disadvantages might include an unavailability of important and necessary sources or discovering that a topic has little historical significance. Other notations might include thoughts about how well your primary and secondary sources support each other. Also, this section is the ideal place to sketch out the significance of your topic.

2. *To Do List*: As you can see from your schedule and checklist, there are a number of details to keep up with. To Do Lists include tasks you need to complete, people responsible for each task, and due dates. The list can also include a list of ideas you want to explore further. For example, you might discover in your research that George Washington especially enjoyed dancing, but your source did not specify the names of dances of the period or titles of songs. At this point, you would want to make to note to follow up on this idea.

3. *Context*: As you proceed with your work, note information you discover that increases your understanding of your topic's historical framework. Describe the ideas and values of the period, the geographic influences, and the social and cultural influences of your topic. Record how these are working together to complete the points you want to make in your historical paper and how you can depict this framework in your visual project. Make note of any gaps you have in these areas and note when you have closed the gaps.

4. *Sources*: Record the sources you use in your research in Turabian style. Note if the entry is a primary or secondary source. Take careful notes about the information from each source. You might use a variety of colored highlighters to indicate information that refers to each of the elements of the historical framework and your topic's historical significance. Remember that you will need to include an annotated bibliography with your historic paper, so having these notes as a reference will be valuable to you. Also, using this section of your journal to make these notes will help you stay with your schedule. When you write your paper, everything you will want to include will be in this one place.

5. *Contacts*: Some of your sources will include people and places. Use this section to record names, e-mail address, mailing addresses, Web sites, and telephone and fax numbers. A written list is particularly useful if you need to contact someone several times.

# CHAPTER 5

# Writing Historical Papers

The next step in the CATCH process is writing the historical paper. Your students will have completed their research and filled their journals with relevant information. They are well equipped to begin writing. This chapter addresses the steps that students need to take in writing their papers, including assembling their research data into a manageable form, creating a title that captures a topic's significance, constructing an introduction based on a premise, developing points that support the premise, forming a conclusion, and refining the draft product. For a summary of the building blocks that make up a successful historical paper, see Figure 19.

## Assembling Data Into a Manageable Form

During this stage, the journals will be of great help to your students. For example, if they have written their guiding questions and answers to these questions in the Notations section, they can comb their notes for relevant information to use for identifying and formulating points to support the premise of their papers. The data will probably be jumbled, so as an organizational tool, students could use a highlighting system to sort the information that relates to each supporting point. Details that relate to the first point could be highlighted in yellow, the second point in green, and the third point in orange. When students begin to write the body of their papers, they could analyze the highlighted parts as they sift through their data and decide on the most relevant and persuasive information.

In the Contents section of their journals, students will have collected abundant information about their topics' historical framework elements: ideas

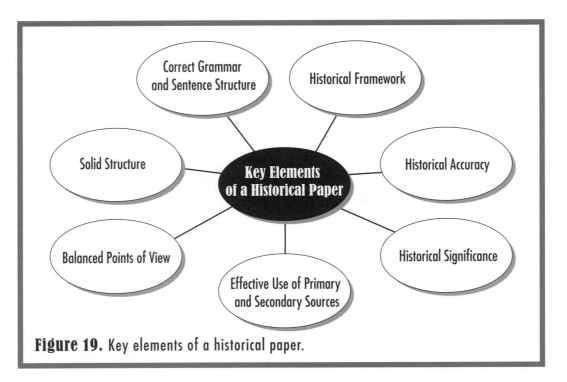

**Figure 19.** Key elements of a historical paper.

and values of the period, geographical influences, social issues, and cultural issues. If they placed their data in these categories as they progressed in their research, the information should already be somewhat organized. For a fishbone graphic organizer that lets students view their key points in each of these elements, see Figures 20 and 21. Once students have completed the fishbone, they will be able to use it as a reference and as a reminder of the elements they need to include in their historical papers.

To connect the information in the Notations and Contents sections, students could use the same highlighting system. For example, one piece of information in the Ideas and Values category might relate to supporting point one, so students would highlight the data in yellow to correspond with the first point. Another idea in that category might fit with point three, so students would highlight that detail in orange.

With this method of matching information about the supporting points and about the elements of the historical framework of their topics, students will be able weave to their data together to create a historical paper in the manner of a historian.

# Creating a Title That Captures the Topic's Significance

During the research and writing stages of their projects, students might have referred to their topics by a working title, such as the Battle of Bull Run

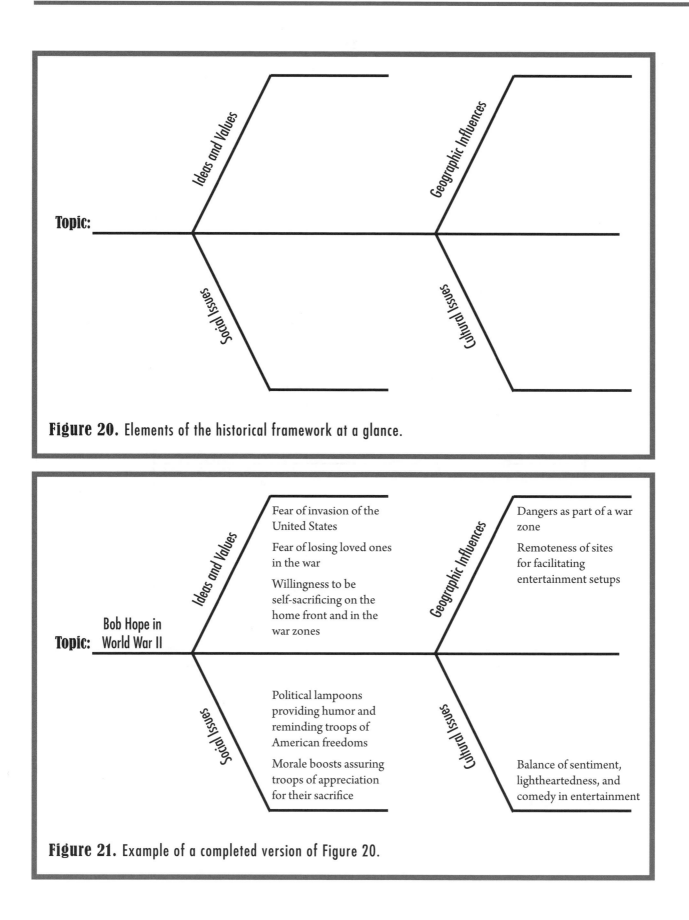

**Figure 20.** Elements of the historical framework at a glance.

**Figure 21.** Example of a completed version of Figure 20.

paper or the Indonesian Dutch paper. This kind of title helps students think about their work, but they know that at some point, they will need to select a final title. Selecting a true title might not come until the paper's completion, but whenever it comes, it should speak of the topic's significance. The premise statement is a good reference for creating a title.

Some examples of titles that hint at a topic's significance include:

**Premise:** At a crucial time for American Forces in the Pacific, a group of Navajos developed and implemented the most significant military code used during World War II.

**Possible Title:** "How an Unbreakable Code Saved Innumerable Lives"

**Premise:** The decision to use the atomic bomb had the greatest impact of any decision the American government made during the 20th century.

**Possible Title:** "The Blast That Lasts: Effects of Dropping the Atomic Bomb"

**Premise:** Bob Hope played a significant role in boosting the morale of U.S. troops stationed in combat zones during World War II through his commitment to bringing entertaining shows and by assuring his audience that they were fighting to save the American way of life and values.

**Possible Title:** "The Hope That Bob Brought"

A catchy title draws interest to a paper, which is useful, but students should keep in mind that their title is the first acquaintance readers have with a topic. It is important for students to create a title that not only invites a reader to learn about a subject but also introduces a topic's significance.

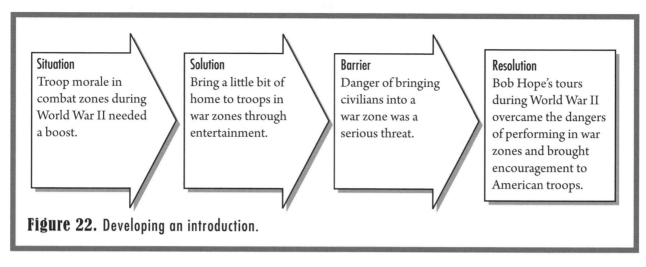

**Situation**
Troop morale in combat zones during World War II needed a boost.

**Solution**
Bring a little bit of home to troops in war zones through entertainment.

**Barrier**
Danger of bringing civilians into a war zone was a serious threat.

**Resolution**
Bob Hope's tours during World War II overcame the dangers of performing in war zones and brought encouragement to American troops.

**Figure 22.** Developing an introduction.

# Constructing an Introduction Based on a Premise

The most important part of an introduction is the premise statement, also commonly known as a topic sentence. Sometimes this statement is all an introduction needs. At other times, an idea in the premise needs elaboration. There is not a specific formula for constructing an introduction. Students can use their imaginations and their sense of their topic's significance to introduce a paper.

Although there is no specific formula for writing an introduction, here is a format to consider using: Present a situation, followed by a solution to the situation, then a barrier to activating the solution, and finally the resolution, which includes the premise. An introduction to a paper about Bob Hope's work in World War II provides an example of implementing this plan (see Figure 22).

Using this model, an introduction to a historical paper titled "The Hope That Bob Brought" could unfold as follows (note that the italicized sentence is the premise statement previously created):

Fear, loneliness, and being surrounded by the horrors of war can be so discouraging to a soldier that continuing to fight with energy seems useless. High morale is essential to the well-being of soldiers in a combat zone of a war. World War II was exceptionally taxing on the morale of American servicemen and women. From North Africa to the Pacific Islands, the troops needed a lift to their spirits and their motivation to keep trying. In the early stages of World War II, Bob Hope, a renowned comedian, saw how entertainment could make a significant difference to people in combat zones, and he began to work on bringing shows to troops stationed in these critical areas. Because the dangers for civilian personnel entering and leaving these zones were great, Bob Hope had to convince authorities that his mission would be worth all of the risks. He did so, and the enterprise turned out to be of greater success than anyone could have anticipated. *Bob Hope played a significant role in boosting the morale of U.S. troops stationed in combat zones during World War II through his commitment to bringing entertaining shows and by assuring his audience that they were fighting to save the American way of life and values.*

However the student chooses to compose his or her introduction, it should include the premise statement and set up the significance of the historical paper's topic.

## Developing Supporting Points

The body of a historical paper is made up of points designed to persuade the reader that the assertion declared in the premise statement is reasonable to accept. When students analyze their research data, several points will emerge. At that time, students need to decide on three or four points and rank them in order of their impact and then decide whether to present the points in a descending or ascending order. A descending order places the most convincing point first while an ascending order places the most convincing point last.

Because the supporting points comprise the body of the paper, they have the load of carrying major components of a historical paper. These components include supporting the premise statement, applying the elements of the topic's historical framework, weaving together primary and secondary sources, and presenting balanced viewpoints. Worksheets 5 and 6 in Appendix A (see pp. 147–148) address this challenge to students. Worksheet 5 is a blank graphic organizer for students to complete as a sketch of how they can integrate these components in the body of their historical papers. Worksheet 6 is an example of how to complete and use the graphic organizer. Students should be given both the blank graphic organizer and the completed one when they are prepared to begin developing their supporting points.

## Forming a Conclusion

The supporting points and their elaboration prepare the reader for a conclusion that clenches the assertion of the premise statement. Basically, the conclusion summarizes the main idea of the introduction and emphasizes the premise statement by alluding to it with emphasis and conviction. Here is an example of a possible conclusion for the historical paper "The Hope That Bob Brought."

> The deep significance of Bob Hope's contributions to servicemen and women and their anxious families back home during World War II is evident by the many tributes people made to Bob Hope during the war and in the years since World War II. Major acknowledgements signifying the importance of his work have continued to come even 50 years after his first show for combat troops. He was 93 years old when he accepted his last award. Bob Hope's theme song was "Thanks for the Memories." And, the gratitude was definitely mutual. Veterans of World War II are still thanking Bob Hope for the memories of bringing encouragement and a bit of comic relief during the fearful and tumultuous times of a fierce and devastating war.

Though the conclusion is brief, it captures the significance of the premise and gives value to the topic.

# Refining the Work

Students need to reflect on their work and refine it at every stage. Refinement or revising involves making changes as students see how to strengthen their points and tighten their premise statements and conclusions. Correcting grammatical errors and checking for clarity of communication is also important. It is helpful to pair students to read each other's papers to give feedback about clarity and logical flow of ideas. It will benefit students to give them time to refine and revise so that they can create their best possible product.

Grading student work is always a concern to teachers. Figure 23 is a rubric you might want to use as a summative evaluation of your students' historical papers. You should give this document to your students before they begin their project so that they will know their precise expectations and can use it as a guide in their refinement analysis.

In the CATCH approach, writing a historical paper before constructing a visual project is essential because the process helps students understand the significance of their topics and gives them a strong sense of the reality of the people and events they portray. This intense investigation also equips students to instill an appreciation of their topics in those who read their papers and view their visual projects. What an impressive accomplishment for you and your students!

| Rating | Historical Quality | Research Quality | Presentation Quality |
|---|---|---|---|
| 4 (Highest Level) | • Facts are historically accurate and verifiable through sources cited.<br>• Historical framework is complete and relevant.<br>  ▸ Ideas and values of the time period are fully developed.<br>  ▸ Geographical influences are explained and well connected to events.<br>  ▸ Social issues are explained and well connected to events.<br>  ▸ Cultural issues are explained and well connected to events.<br>• Historical significance is well established and the topic's impact is clear. | • Uses a wide variety of categories of sources appropriate for the topic's premise (i.e., Internet, interviews, newspaper and magazine articles, reference materials, etc.)<br>• Uses and cites an appropriate number of sources within each category of sources.<br>• Uses many available primary sources relevant to the topic's premise.<br>• Effectively organizes information gathered from sources.<br>• Takes thorough notes from sources.<br>• Includes all necessary bibliographical information for each source. | • States the topic's premise clearly.<br>• Effectively supports the topic's premise.<br>• Draws a reasonable and clearly stated conclusion based on relevant supporting evidence.<br>• Presents a balanced point of view.<br>• Primary and secondary sources effectively support each other.<br>• Clearly communicates points and is well organized.<br>• Grammar and style are correct.<br>• Bibliography is appropriately annotated.<br>• Sources are correctly entered into the bibliography. |
| 3 | • Facts are historically accurate and verifiable through sources cited.<br>• Historical framework is somewhat complete and relevant.<br>  ▸ Ideas and values of the time period are developed.<br>  ▸ Geographical influences are explained and connected to events.<br>  ▸ Social issues are explained and connected to events.<br>  ▸ Cultural issues are explained and connected to events.<br>• Historical significance is established and the topic's impact is clear. | • Uses a variety of categories of sources appropriate for the topic's premise (i.e., Internet, interviews, newspaper and magazine articles, reference materials, etc.).<br>• Uses and cites a large number of sources within each category of sources.<br>• Uses several primary sources relevant to the topic's premise.<br>• Clearly organizes information gathered from sources.<br>• Takes adequate notes from sources.<br>• Includes all necessary bibliographical information for each source. | • States the topic's premise clearly.<br>• Adequately supports the topic's premise.<br>• Draws a reasonable and clearly stated conclusion based on relevant supporting evidence.<br>• Presents a balanced point of view.<br>• Primary and secondary sources usually support each other.<br>• Communication is understandable and is well organized.<br>• Grammar and style are correct.<br>• Bibliography is annotated.<br>• Sources are correctly entered into the bibliography. |

**Figure 23.** Rubric for grading and critiquing historical papers.

| Rating | Historical Quality | Research Quality | Presentation Quality |
|---|---|---|---|
| 2 | • Facts are limited and somewhat historically accurate.<br>• Historical framework is addressed.<br>▸ Ideas and values of the time period are mentioned.<br>▸ Geographical influences are mentioned.<br>▸ Social issues are mentioned.<br>▸ Cultural issues are mentioned.<br>• Historical significance is partially established. | • Uses few categories of sources appropriate for the topic's premise (i.e., Internet, interviews, newspaper and magazine articles, reference materials, etc.).<br>• Uses and cites few sources within some of the categories of sources.<br>• Uses few primary sources relevant to the topic's premise.<br>• Somewhat organizes information gathered from sources.<br>• Takes limited notes from sources.<br>• Includes some of the bibliographical information from each source. | • States the topic's premise vaguely.<br>• Somewhat supports the topic's premise.<br>• Draws a conclusion but is not clearly based on relevant supporting evidence.<br>• Presents a single point of view.<br>• Primary and secondary sources used in an unrelated fashion.<br>• Communication and organization are vague.<br>• Grammar and style are occasionally incorrect.<br>• Bibliography is sketchily annotated.<br>• Sources are haphazardly entered into the bibliography. |
| 1 | • Facts are unsupported.<br>• Historical framework is unclear.<br>▸ Ideas and values of the time period are vague or absent.<br>▸ Geographical influences are vague or absent.<br>▸ Social issues are vague or absent.<br>▸ Cultural issues are vague or absent.<br>• Historical significance is unclear. | • Uses one or two categories of sources appropriate for the topic (i.e., Internet, interviews, newspaper and magazine articles, reference materials, etc.).<br>• Uses and cites several sources within each category of sources.<br>• Uses one or no primary source.<br>• Organization of information gathered from sources is unclear.<br>• Takes few notes from sources.<br>• Includes little bibliographical information for each source. | • Introduction does not state a premise.<br>• Paper does not come to a conclusion.<br>• Does not mention a point of view.<br>• Sources are vague and unrelated.<br>• Communication is unclear.<br>• Grammar and style are often incorrect.<br>• Bibliography is not annotated.<br>• Sources are incorrectly and incompletely entered into the bibliography. |

# CHAPTER 6

# Constructing Visual Projects

Creating and showing a visual project for a history event is an exciting venture. The CATCH approach gives students an opportunity to demonstrate both an understanding of a topic and a talent for bringing that understanding to life. Hopefully, by the time students write their papers, create their visual projects, and present their work for the public at your history fair, they will have a broader understanding of history and a feeling of accomplishment.

As you and your students enter the process of constructing visual projects, you will be helping your students with several undertakings, including connecting their visual projects to their historical papers, developing their projects, refining their projects, and presenting their projects to the public.

Encourage students to keep in mind the importance of producing a quality product in every phase of their work. For example, if their work includes writing or speaking, students need to use correct grammar and spelling where applicable. They also need to take care to construct visuals with correctly aligned pieces and use decorating schemes that are pleasant to observe and that help portray their topics. If students create a model, they will want to be certain to construct it to scale for historical accuracy. The tips included throughout this chapter provide guidelines for quality construction of each of the visual projects discussed.

## Connecting Visual Projects to Historical Papers

Visual projects help bring the people and events of the past to life. Historical papers pave the way for this to happen by showing the reality of people involved

## Table 7
## Examples of Converting Historical Paper Topics to Projects

TOPIC: Bob Hope's USO Tours in World War II

- *Exhibits:* Include the premise statement at the beginning of the display and the conclusion at the end. Fill the space in between with captioned photographs, maps, quotes, and other appropriate documents. Provide a CD player that plays songs of the day and excerpts from one of Bob Hope's shows.

- *Scrapbooks:* Pretend to be a soldier, a loved one on the Home Front, or a member of the cast or crew traveling with Bob Hope and create a collection of documents about Bob Hope's tours such as magazine and newspaper articles, letters from people who attended a show, and images and documents about war activity in pertinent vicinities. These documents would have been cited and used as sources in the historic paper. Use paper and trim that match the theme of your scrapbook.

- *Performances:* Reenact one of Hope's real shows with people playing Bob Hope and any other of the entertainers that matches the talent of the students in the group: stand-up comics, singers, and dancers.

- *Media Presentations:* Create a Web site that links appropriate sites about Bob Hope's work in World War II and information about the war that shows the need for boosting morale. Develop a multimedia presentation with scenes, sounds, and text about Bob Hope's World War II tours. Include a video of a personal interview of a serviceman or woman who attended or listened by radio to one of Bob Hope's shows during the war. Weave in the premise and conclusion of the historic paper. Use information in the sources from the paper.

in the events of a topic. Therefore, it is important for a paper and project to make a strong connection so that people who view students' visual projects can grasp that reality. Some examples of how students can make connections between specific paper topics and projects are included in Table 7.

Many categories of visual projects facilitate ways to demonstrate the components of historical papers. If a project does not provide a means of communicating a paper's premise, historical significance, or historical framework, students might want to post an informational poster on an easel beside a model or demonstration project to provide an outline of these important elements.

To check students' understanding of how to connect a historical paper and a visual project, have students read the play, "A Ghostly Gift," included in Appendix C (see p. 161) and take notes on the chart in Worksheet 7 (located in Appendix A; see p. 149) as they read. This worksheet gives students a means of recording their observations about the premise, historical significance, and historical framework of the topic of the play. To reinforce the concept of connecting a historical paper and a visual project, follow up this activity by conducting a class discussion using the answer key for Worksheet 7, provided in Appendix B.

# Developing Visual Projects

This section gives detailed information about developing visual projects. As the students begin their work, you might want to give them a rubric that clarifies the standards of quality for each project category. This rubric can also serve as a guide to you for evaluating your students' work. Each section below contains a sample rubric for evaluating each type of visual project: Exhibits, Scrapbooks, and Posters; Models and Dioramas; Performances; and Media Presentations. Each of these types are discussed and sample projects are shown in the sections that follow.

## EXHIBITS, SCRAPBOOKS, AND POSTERS

This category of visual projects challenges students to combine hands-on artistry with a talent for selecting a few words to express deep concepts. You might need to guide students toward understanding how to capture the historical framework and historical significance of their topics through this medium.

A rubric for evaluating student exhibits, scrapbooks, and posters is included in Figure 24.

### Exhibits

Exhibits are popular among students, and they are fun to construct. You might want to set height and width requirements depending on the space you will use for displays. You might also want to set a maximum number of words that students can use in captions, titles, and comments so that images dominate the exhibits rather than text. For an example of a student-created exhibit, see Figure 25.

The following are some tips for creating exhibits that you'll want to share with your students interested in this form of visual project.

1. Use materials that are consistent with the topic. For example, if the exhibit is about ancient Egypt, you might use background paper or fabric that suggests desert sands and a border of oasis palms or Egyptian designs. The shapes of the background paper for captions, the selection of font used

| Rating | Historical Quality | Presentation Quality |
|---|---|---|
| 4 (highest level) | • Accurately represents the events and concepts of the historical paper.<br>• Strongly reflects the historical framework of the topic.<br>• Strongly reflects the historical significance of the topic. | • Design contributes to the spirit and theme of the content of the topic.<br>• Images and captions capture the concepts of the topic.<br>• Presentation of material is appealing.<br>• Written material uses grammar correctly and appropriately. |
| 3 | • Represents the events and concepts of the historical paper somewhat accurately.<br>• Somewhat reflects the historical framework of the topic.<br>• Somewhat reflects the historical significance of the topic. | • Design adequately reflects the spirit and theme of the content of the topic.<br>• Images and captions are appropriate for the concepts of the topic.<br>• Presentation of material is interesting.<br>• Written material uses grammar correctly and appropriately. |
| 2 | • Represents the events and concepts of the historical paper with limited accuracy.<br>• Refers to the historical framework of the topic.<br>• Refers to the historical significance of the topic. | • Design alludes to the spirit and theme of the content of the topic.<br>• Images and captions refer to the concepts of the topic.<br>• Presentation of material is adequate.<br>• Written material somewhat uses grammar correctly and appropriately. |
| 1 | • Haphazardly represents the events and concepts of the historical paper.<br>• Ignores or misrepresents the historical framework of the topic.<br>• Ignores or misrepresents the historical significance of the topic. | • Design is inconsistent with the spirit and theme of the content of the topic.<br>• Images and captions are incomplete in regard to the concepts of the topic.<br>• Presentation of material is bland.<br>• Written material often uses grammar incorrectly and/or inappropriately. |

**Figure 24.** Rubric for evaluating a visual project: Exhibits, scrapbooks, and posters.

for wording, and the overall color scheme can also help communicate the topic's concepts. For example, in an exhibit about quilts that gave secret codes to slaves escaping through the Underground Railroad, quilt squares could serve as a background and quilt patterns could serve as shapes for writing information.

3. Use supplemental materials that enhance the exhibit. Music from a CD player is an excellent way to make the exhibit's topic come alive. Hands-on activities are effective if they are appropriate to the topic. For example, if the topic is about the impact of the Morse code on communications, you might set up a telegraph with a portion of the code for reference. People who visit the exhibit could then practice tapping out brief messages.

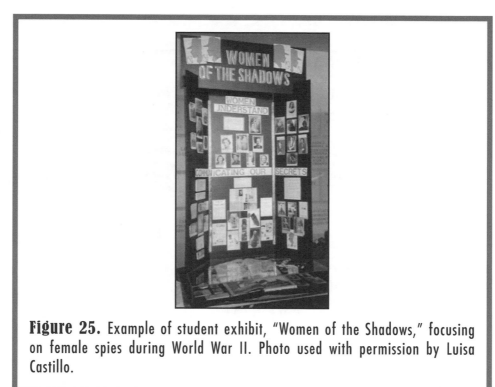

**Figure 25.** Example of student exhibit, "Women of the Shadows," focusing on female spies during World War II. Photo used with permission by Luisa Castillo.

4. Use information and images consistent with the historical framework of the historical paper. For example, if the topic deals with implements used in ancient Roman households, you would not want to include pictures of items not yet invented, such as grandfather clocks.
5. Check all grammar and spelling usage so that the display is scholarly and appropriate for an academic presentation.

## Scrapbooks

This visual project is similar to photo albums, but it includes small additions of explanatory text. Scrapbooks are among the best avenues to connect with people of the past in a personal way, but generally require a lot of hard work (cutting, gluing, organizing) and some patient skill and creativity. The example in Figure 26 is of a scrapbook constructed by a student taking the persona of a maid living on a 17th century farm in England.

The following are some tips you'll want to share with students who are interested in creating scrapbooks for their visual projects.

1. Use materials that reflect the theme of the scrapbook. For example, bamboo place mats could serve as covers for a scrapbook about China or you could use red, white, and blue bunting for a scrapbook with an American theme. Scatter real or simulated items of interest related to your topic throughout the book such as cotton bolls, pieces of lace, shards of pottery,

## EXAMPLE OF A SCRAPBOOK COVER

1. Wool fabric background
2. Parchment or old-looking paper
3. Appropriate font
4. Collage of work images
5. Wool yarn to bind the book

## SAMPLE PAGE OF OUTSIDE WORK

1. Light brown paper to align with garden soil
2. Maid in 17th-century clothing
3. Flower that grows in an English garden
4. Picture of vegetables
5. Parchment or old-looking background paper
6. Picture of an English garden

## SAMPLE PAGE OF INSIDE WORK

1. Soiled scrubbing cloth
2. Gray paper to align with grime in the fireplace
3. Picture of a sooty fireplace with laundry and 17th-century implements
4. Parchment or old-looking background paper
5. Maid daydreaming of a different life

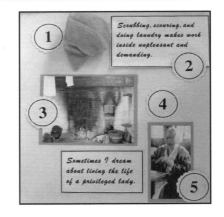

**Figure 26.** Sample scrapbook pages.

fabric scraps, small items of jewelry, fragments of bones, or candle wax stamped with a significant seal.

2. Shape the scrapbook to match its theme if a shape is appropriate. If your book is about a certain bridge, make the cover and each page the shape of a bridge. Other appropriate shapes might include buildings and landmarks such as castles or the Statue of Liberty.

3. Pretend that someone from the past has compiled the scrapbook. Let this person's identity show through in captions with pictures or in brief explanations about a scene. For example, if you are pretending to be Nancy Reagan, wife of former President Ronald Reagan, include her name on the title page: "A First Lady's Impression of America" by Nancy Reagan. One of the pictures could be of her and the President, and the caption might read, "Ronnie and I welcoming our first guests to the White House."

4. Make sure the scrapbook is manageable for people to examine. Secure the pages together well. You might choose to use a bound commercial scrapbook, but if you use special materials, you will need to hold it together with sturdy and reliable fasteners. Arrange supplementary items so that the book is not too bulky to handle.

5. Be consistent in the theme. For example, you would not want to mix satin and burlap on a page about the wardrobe of Marie Antoinette.

6. Use text judiciously. As far as possible, let visuals tell the story.

7. Apply subtle borders to pages and images to enhance them without overwhelming your work.

8. Be neat. Trim your pictures evenly or use shape-cutters. Avoid leaving glue or tape peeking beyond your images.

## Posters

Students will be able to communicate significant information on a single poster board if they plan their design with thought and care. You might want to supply an outline to ensure that students adequately reflect the historical framework and historical significance of their historical papers. Figure 27 provides an example of a poster that uses graphs to provide important statistical information.

The following are tips for constructing posters.

1. Meet the challenge of reflecting the historical paper on the small field of a poster board by emphasizing the heart of the topic. For example, you might highlight all or part of your historical framework, or you might write your premise statement and conclusion of your work.

2. Be selective with illustrations so that they are the most representative pieces you can use to reflect your topic.

3. Be neat. If you use pictures, trim them evenly or use shape-cutters. Avoid leaving glue or tape peeking beyond your images.

4. Be selective with text. Too many words can keep a viewer from taking an interest in the message. For example, your poster might highlight the contributions of a significant leader, so you would list his or her accomplishments. For variety, consider using a symbol to represent each item on the list and place the appropriate visual beside the appropriate text. Lists do

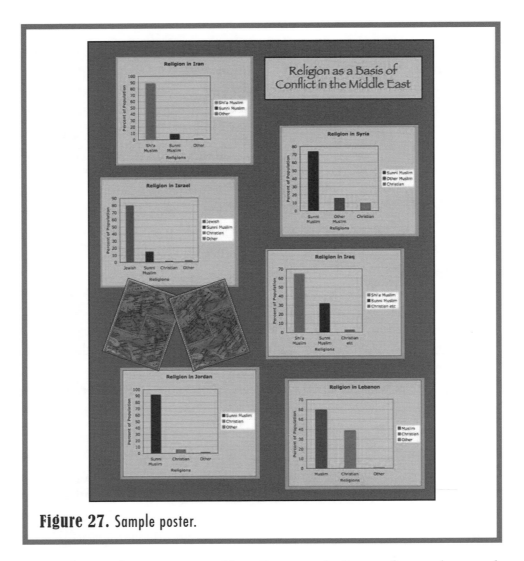

**Figure 27.** Sample poster.

not have to be in a sequential line. Items on the list can form a shape such as a triangle or be randomly scattered across the poster board.

5. Use a background that reflects your message. Although the background should not overpower the poster, it can serve an effective purpose. Enlarged photographs are functional. Watermark them so that they do not stand out but they help support the primary pieces of your poster. Maps also are appropriate backgrounds.

6. Using a variety of materials such as various textures of paper, colored streamers, and small, lightweight artifacts can enhance your theme, but you do not want these additions to be too busy. For example, if your poster is about Lincoln's second inaugural address, you might drape the top of your poster with a narrow swath of red, white, and blue bunting. Or, if your topic is about Japan, you might scatter a few origami items across your poster.

## MODELS AND DIORAMAS

Accuracy in scale and imagery is key in constructing models and dioramas. Encourage students to represent their structures and scenes from authentic diagrams and other appropriate images. Materials also are important to replicate with accuracy. Obviously students cannot use real gold for a building's dome, but other materials can give a reasonable appearance of gold. In the scenes of the dioramas, remind students that they need to use authentic pieces. For example, Crusaders did not carry rifles. A rubric for evaluating models and dioramas is included in Figure 28.

The following tips will be useful to your students as they undertake the process of building models and dioramas.

1. Communicate the significance of the structure with a supplemental sign. You might want to include the premise statement or the conclusion of your historical paper. Other helpful supplemental additions might include floor plans of buildings or diagrams that show change over time, such as various positions of troops at different stages in a battle.

2. Be certain your work is historically accurate. Study diagrams, maps, and pictures to help you represent your subject in a true sense. If you have a clear understanding of the purpose and use of your structure, you will be able to establish accuracy. For example, if you create a diorama of a battlefield, you will want to understand how the terrain of the field made a difference in the challenges facing the battle strategists, as well as the people carrying on the fight. You will want to know how many people were fighting on each side and know their positions at some stage of the battle. If your model is a castle, you will want to know who lived in it and what significant events took place there. You also will want to understand the purposes of the rooms, open areas, and outbuildings.

3. Carefully construct your model or diorama so that it is neat and pleasing to view. For example, avoid having dried glue oozing from cracks or crooked windows that are supposed to be straight. An example of neat and eye-catching models is found in Figure 29, which presents a picture of two award-winning student models—one of a Spanish mission and one of St. Isaac's Cathedral in St. Petersburg, Russia.

4. Mentally put yourself in the place of someone who would have participated in your model or diorama so that you can get a good sense of the place and be able to communicate that idea to those who view your work. Try to imagine what it would have been like to be part of erecting a cathedral, defending a fortress, or climbing a slope with bullets whizzing all around you.

| Rating | Historical Quality | Presentation Quality |
|---|---|---|
| 4 (highest level) | • Accurately represents the events and concepts of the historical paper.<br>• Strongly reflects the historical framework of the topic.<br>• Strongly reflects the historical significance of the topic. | • Structure or scene strongly adheres to a proportional scale.<br>• Supplementary poster captures the central concepts of the historical framework and the historical significance.<br>• Materials in the design are consistent with the structure or scene.<br>• A picture and/or diagram affixed to the poster clearly authenticates the accuracy of the representation of the structure or scene. |
| 3 | • Represents the events and concepts of the historical paper somewhat accurately.<br>• Somewhat reflects the historical framework of the topic.<br>• Somewhat reflects the historical significance of the topic. | • Structure or scene closely adheres to a proportional scale.<br>• Supplementary poster adequately reflects the central concepts of the historical framework and the historical significance.<br>• Materials in the design are reasonably consistent with the structure or scene.<br>• A picture and/or diagram affixed to the poster reasonably authenticates the accuracy of the representation of the structure or scene. |
| 2 | • Represents the events and concepts of the historical paper with limited accuracy.<br>• Refers to the historical framework of the topic.<br>• Refers to the historical significance of the topic. | • Structure or scene somewhat adheres to a proportional scale.<br>• Supplementary poster sketches the central concepts of the historical framework and the historical significance.<br>• Materials in the design are moderately consistent with the structure or scene.<br>• A picture and/or diagram affixed to the poster somewhat reflects the accuracy of the representation of the structure or scene. |
| 1 | • Haphazardly represents the events and concepts of the historical paper.<br>• Ignores or misrepresents the historical framework of the topic.<br>• Ignores or misrepresents the historical significance of the topic. | • Structure or scene follows no particularly proportional scale.<br>• Supplementary poster is vague or absent.<br>• Materials in the design are inconsistent with the structure or scene.<br>• A picture and/or diagram of the representation of the structure or scene is sketchy or absent. |

**Figure 28.** Rubric for evaluating a visual project: Models and dioramas.

**Figure 29.** Examples of two award-winning models. Photo used with permission by Julie Greene.

## PERFORMANCES

Students can probe deeply into the past and carry audiences with them through demonstrations, plays, monologues, storytelling, speeches, reenactments, and virtual historical trials. Performances give students the opportunity to put themselves in the hearts and minds of real people of the past who have shaped the world students currently occupy. A rubric for evaluating performances is included in Figure 30.

### Demonstrations

Usually, participation in a demonstration involves one of two activities. One of these is teaching others how to construct items people made in the past. The second activity is explaining to viewers how people of the past used certain artifacts. For example, some of the crafts students might construct include basket weaving, making dolls from cornhusks and fabric scraps, or flint knapping, the art of making arrowheads and spear points. Some of the possible demonstrations using artifacts include using a butter churn, demonstrating a stereopticon, or using a metate to grind corn. Demonstrations also can involve arranged presentations of multiple artifacts in a historical setting, with students on hand to discuss their uses and meanings, such as the example in Figure 31.

The following are tips for creating or putting together a demonstration.

1. Display a poster outlining your historical paper to help viewers understand how and why people of the past used your artifacts. Include your premise statement, a sentence to summarize each of your supporting points, and your conclusion.
2. Wear costumes that reflect the people who used your artifacts. This helps bring realism to your demonstration.

| Rating | Historical Quality | Presentation Quality |
|---|---|---|
| 4 (highest level) | • Accurately represents the events and concepts of the historical paper.<br>• Strongly reflects the historical framework of the topic.<br>• Strongly reflects the historical significance of the topic. | • Costumes, sets, and/or props contribute to the spirit and theme of the content of the topic.<br>• Participant is well prepared and delivers material flawlessly.<br>• Content of material is appealing.<br>• Participant delivers material with sparkling energy.<br>• Participant uses grammar correctly and appropriately. |
| 3 | • Represents the events and concepts of the historical paper somewhat accurately.<br>• Somewhat reflects the historical framework of the topic.<br>• Somewhat reflects the historical significance of the topic. | • Costumes, sets, and/or props are appropriate for the topic.<br>• Participant is somewhat well prepared and delivers material with few mistakes.<br>• Content of material is interesting.<br>• Participant delivers material with suitable energy.<br>• Participant uses grammar correctly and appropriately. |
| 2 | • Represents the events and concepts of the historical paper with limited accuracy.<br>• Refers to the historical framework of the topic.<br>• Refers to the historical significance of the topic. | • Costumes, sets, and/or props somewhat relate to the topic.<br>• Participant is partially prepared, but delivers material with many mistakes.<br>• Content of material is moderately appropriate.<br>• Participant delivers material with little energy.<br>• Participant uses grammar somewhat correctly and appropriately. |
| 1 | • Haphazardly represents the events and concepts of the historical paper.<br>• Ignores or misrepresents the historical framework of the topic.<br>• Ignores or misrepresents the historical significance of the topic. | • Costumes, sets, and/or props are absent or inappropriate for the topic.<br>• Participant is unprepared and delivers material falteringly.<br>• Content of material lacks inspiration.<br>• Participant delivers material laconically.<br>• Participant uses grammar incorrectly. |

**Figure 30.** Rubric for evaluating a visual project: Performances.

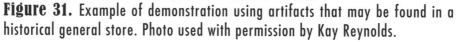

**Figure 31.** Example of demonstration using artifacts that may be found in a historical general store. Photo used with permission by Kay Reynolds.

3. Set up your station to capture the time and place people might have used your artifacts. For example, a semblance of a general store would be a good setting for 19th-century household items.

4. Display a poster of pictures of people using or making your artifacts to assist you in explaining your demonstration.

5. Involve your audience. If conditions are favorable, invite visitors at your station to try to identify and use an artifact as people of the past might have used it. Discuss how and why the artifacts are no longer in use. Challenge your audience to name objects that have replaced obsolete items. For example, a CD player would have replaced a phonograph, and a flashlight or electric lamp would have replaced a lantern. Encourage audiences to appreciate how people of the past lived and how much easier our lives are today because inventors were able to use the artifacts in your display as forerunners in creating items that make our lives more convenient.

## Plays, Skits, and Monologues

Both preparing and performing plays, skits, and monologues are excellent avenues for capturing the ideas and values of a period. Two scripts for plays that reflect historical time periods are found in Appendix C. Students can use these scripts to help write their own.

Writing and performing a play, skit, or monologue is an ideal way to bring history to life for audiences, because these performances provide the opportunity to experience how people felt and acted in their circumstances during a certain time in history. Tips for creating effective plays, skits, and monologues include the following.

1. Capture the reality and importance of the period and the event you represent in your work. Be sure your work reflects the historical framework and significance of your topic and convey those ideas in your dialogue.

2. Write and speak real and believable dialogue. It is best to avoid speaking in an accent if you cannot accurately represent it, but you can achieve realism through your delivery of lines. You also want to avoid imposing today's vernacular on historical figures. For example, Julius Caesar would hardly greet Marc Antony with, "Hey, man! What's up?"

3. Try to understand the character you are portraying so that you can present him or her with accuracy. Woodrow Wilson would require a persona of dignity while Teddy Roosevelt would be animated and robust. Practice so that you neither overact nor underrepresent your character.

4. Let your costumes, sets, and props help you tell your story. These do not have to be elaborate, and you will probably want to keep the sets simple because you might have to move them on and off a performance area quickly.

5. Use artifacts or replicas when possible to give authenticity to your play. For example, people of the 18th century would have written with a quill while people of the mid-19th century would have written with a metal nib inserted into a wooden shaft. Both would have dipped their pens in small inkpots.

6. Don't be afraid to ask for help! Most plays have separate crew teams to help with costumes, sets, props, and setting up the day of the show.

7. Memorize your lines and practice until your performance is smooth and natural.

## Storytelling

Storytelling is an art form that requires a talent for capturing a culture, as well as for telling a good story. A storyteller might tell a legend or myth belonging to a certain group of people, or a storyteller might pretend to be an eyewitness and tell about a certain event he or she experienced. Some points to keep in mind when preparing and delivering a story include:

1. Introduce the story by informing the audience about the culture the story comes out of and how the story fits into that culture. This places the story in a historical framework and helps the audience understand the significance of the account.

2. As far as possible, create an aura fitting to the story. For example, if you are telling a cowboy tale about a trail ride, you might dress like a drover and sit on a log or stump as though you are spinning your yarn around a campfire. You could pretend that you are veteran of many rides and your audience is made up of first time herders.

3. Preface the story with a statement that creates a feeling of reality. For example, you might tell an Apache legend about how Red Fox tricked the fireflies, stole their fire, and spread it around the Earth for people to use. You could

begin by saying, "I know this story is true because my great-grandmother told me she always made her fires for cooking stew from a coal she kept burning from the time Red Fox left it there many years ago." You audience will know that you are just telling tales, but your pretense helps make the story sound plausible. Then, lead the audience to understand how the story reflects the Apache culture.

4. If conditions are appropriate, involve the audience in the story. For example, you might pretend to be a certain Pony Express rider telling about your adventurous route. You could distribute large pictures to people ahead of time and ask them to stand beside you and show the pictures as you progress in your story. Some of the pictures could include your horse, a typical way station where you picked up your mail and ate a meal, a desert scene, a rattlesnake you might have battled, and a campfire.

## Speeches

Giving a speech is an excellent way to present the content of a historical paper because all speeches have an introduction, supporting points, and a conclusion. Through the delivery of a speech, students have an opportunity to bring their paper to life.

First, students must determine if their speech will be informative or persuasive. Informative speeches are designed to explain or report on an event or a condition of a project or organization and have a specific purpose. For example, the purpose of the State of the Union Address by the President of the United States is to inform Congress about how issues and various ventures are developing in the country. Persuasive speeches are designed to convince an audience to take action on a certain issue or to believe a certain idea. For example, a historical paper might have been about the secession of Georgia from the Union. The speech could be an effort to persuade the delegates of the Georgia "Secession Convention" either to secede or not to secede from the Union. Students would speak from the standpoint of a real person who lived during the event associated with their topic. A speech is of their creation, constructed from information acquired when they researched their historical paper.

Some tips for constructing and making speeches include:

1. Identify the audience. On some occasions, the audience might be people living at the present time. For example, you might try to persuade a group to vote for your candidate to become the next United States President to be carved into Mt. Rushmore. Your historical paper might have been about the contributions of Woodrow Wilson, so your speech would bring out the supporting points you made in your historical paper. If the setting of your speech takes place in the past, draw your listeners into the time period by addressing them as an audience of the past. For example,

you might begin a speech about Georgia secession by saying, "My fellow Georgians, we will soon have a momentous decision to make: Whether to stay with the United States or to join the recently formed Confederate States of America. Your vote is vital to the cause!" From that point, you would try to persuade people to secede or not to secede from the Union.

2. Practice your delivery. It is important to enunciate and communicate clearly. Make sure you have stated what your topic is about in your introduction. Tie all of your points to that opening statement, and conclude with a sentence that emphasizes your main idea. Delivering your speech without reading it or referring to notes is ideal. However, if you feel that you cannot do this, read with a variety of voice inflections and make eye contact with your audience as often as possible. Think of yourself as speaking with your audience, not at them or to them.

3. Enhance the presentation. Wearing an appropriate costume helps the audience identify with your time period and topic. Props that are large enough for the audience to see also can help make the points of your speech clear. For example, if you make a speech about funereal practices of ancient Egyptians, you might have a table beside you containing replicas of items found in a pharaoh's tomb. You could hold up each one as you mention it in your speech. If your speaking area is favorable, use visual aids such as large maps or a computer presentation to emphasize and clarify the points of your speech.

## Reenactments

Reenactments require a deep knowledge of the people and circumstances involved in a given event. Some of the most effective events to reenact include battles, the foundation of a town, a meeting such as the Constitutional Convention, historical trials, and lifestyles of certain groups such as mountain men at a Rendezvous. Reenactments are different from plays in that they capture a specific event by showing exactly what happened without developing a plot. For example, in reenacting a battle, troop stations are identified and arranged as realistically as possible (see Figure 32). If dialogue is used, the speakers repeat statements actually spoken at the battle. The battle ensues as it actually happened with people falling on the field, medics racing to aid the wounded, and combatants overcoming real or simulated obstacles as they appeared in the original battle. In a historical trial, students take on the roles of the original prosecutors, defenders, judge, jury, and witnesses. The verdict is the same as in the real trial. The challenge is to re-create the original trial. More about historical trials is included in the next section.

Several tips to keep in mind as you conduct a reenactment include:

1. Reenactments are all about accuracy. Wear costumes and use appropriate artifacts. Facsimiles are fine as long as they resemble the real objects they

**Figure 32.** Scene from a professional reenactment of a drill at Fort Atkinson, Nebraska. Photo by Helen Bass.

represent. Remove items that people did not use during the time period being depicted. For example, the people you represent might never have seen wristwatches or sneakers.

2. Understand the historical framework and historical significance of the event being reenacted. You might not agree with the people you are portraying, but try to understand why and how they held certain viewpoints and reacted in certain ways. For example, it is difficult for a person in today's time period to understand how the Boston Massacre could have occurred, but if you study both the British soldiers and the colonists' outlooks and understand the background of the conflict, you will be able to bring that incident to life.

3. Use every safety precaution. Schools and other places of performance can have strict rules about firearms and other dangerous items. Do not bring them to the event. If guns are part of your reenactment, they should be replicas. If you reenact the Boston Massacre, use wads of paper for snowballs. Work out ahead of time where the people in the crowd will run when they scatter so that they will not crash into the side of a building or some other harmful obstacle.

4. Strongly consider your venue of presentation. A small room is not conducive to a battle scene, and a vast outdoor arena is a difficult setting for a historical trial.

## Simulations of Historical Trials

Perhaps the most complex of the performances is the virtual historical trial. Students who participate in a Mock Trial program at your school will have had experience in preparing and presenting a trial, but others will find the project more challenging. The tips for conducting a simulation of a historical trial below suggest that students consult a real attorney to advise them on the procedures they intend to follow in their trial presentations. Your students might need your help in finding an attorney willing to donate time for this kind of consultation. Although the virtual historical trial has a format designed to fit its particular style, you and your students can benefit from analyzing the format and tips given in a document titled, "Putting on Mock Trials" by the American Bar Association, found at http://www.abanet.org/publiced/mocktrialguide.pdf.

What if Adolf Hitler had been tried for genocide or Elizabeth Van Lew had been tried by the Confederacy for spying for the Union? What would the verdicts have been? What would have been their sentences? In simulations of historical trials, students prepare and conduct a trial for real people of the past whose activities were questionable enough to possibly warrant a trial, but they were never held accountable for an alleged misdeed. The challenge is to gather and present evidence to both prosecute and defend a defendant. If students choose this medium for a visual project, they will use information they have discovered as they researched their historical paper. Students portraying prosecutors could possibly use the premise and the conclusion of their papers in their opening and closing arguments. The supporting points of their papers will serve as building blocks for their case against the defendant.

Students portraying defense attorneys could turn the premise statement and conclusion of their papers in favor of the defendant and attempt to show how the prosecution's case is faulty at every point. Both attorneys continually will need to keep in mind that it is the prosecution's burden to prove guilt. The defense is responsible for demonstrating to a jury that the prosecution's case leaves reasonable doubt about the guilt of the defendant.

Roles in a historical trial include a judge, one or two prosecuting attorneys, one or two defense attorneys, two witnesses for each side, a clerk, and jury members. If possible, it is best to arrange for a real judge or a lawyer in the community to volunteer to play the judge's role. Give the judge all of the particulars of the case a week or two ahead of time, so that he or she can be familiar with the case. The clerk can be any class member who agrees to serve, because the clerk does not need to be familiar with the case. The clerk swears in the witnesses. The jury can be composed of class members or members of an audience who attend the history fair. You can enlist as many juries as you would like, because it would be interesting to see the level of consistency of their verdicts.

The attorneys must be thoroughly familiar with the case. It would be beneficial if they had researched the historical paper about the defendant as a group. However, another workable plan would be for two groups or two individuals to write separate papers establishing separate premises. For example, one paper could support Elizabeth Van Lew as heroine of the Union cause and worthy of commendation, not condemnation. The other paper could take the

Confederate side and condemn her as a spy deserving the punishment spies have met throughout history: death.

The witnesses need to be familiar with their parts in the case, but they may or may not have written a historical paper about the subject. If they have not researched the topic, the attorneys need to meet with their witnesses and familiarize them with their information. The witnesses could be class members who are willing to read at least one source on the subject as part of the preparation and be willing to participate for fun and friendship.

Table 8 includes a step-by-step listing of the procedures that occur during a historical trial. A good example of how a simulation of a historical trial might play out is included in Appendix C in the script for "The Trial of John C. Calhoun" (see p. 168). Students interested in putting on historical trials may want to read this document to help them gain a better understanding of the trial procedures and appropriate courtroom vocabulary.

General information regarding simulations of historical trials to keep in mind includes:

- *Timing*: Because a virtual historical trial takes place as part of a history fair, it should last no more than one hour. For this reason, the witnesses are limited to two per side, and each part of the trial is limited to a certain set of minutes. A workable schedule gives 5 minutes to each attorney in the opening statements and 5 minutes to each attorney in the closing statements. Eight minutes are set aside for each witness testimony, leaving 8 minutes for the judge's comments and jury deliberation. This schedule is a generic suggestion. After planning your case, you might decide that one witness needs more time than another witness. Before the trial, the prosecution and defense should agree on the length of time their witness testimonies and opening and closing statements should take. Make the total time equal for both sides. Keep each other on track by providing timekeepers. Count cross-examinations for the time of the side asking the questions. For example, time of direct questioning of a prosecution witness is charged to the prosecution team. Time of cross-examining that witness is charged to the defense team.

- *Setting up the courtroom*: Your mock courtroom should be arranged to represent a real courtroom as much as possible. Figure 33 shows a good example of how a courtroom should be arranged.

- *Demeanor of the attorneys*: The attorneys sit during the trial. The defendant sits with the defense attorney. However, attorneys stand during these occasions: delivering opening and closing statements, handing a

## Table 8
## Step-by-Step Procedures for Simulations of Historical Trials

1. A student serves as an announcer and presents a brief historical context for the trial so that the audience will understand the basis for the events that have prompted the trial. (The author(s) of the historical paper writes the introduction, but the spokesperson can either be a member of the trial team or a volunteer.)

2. The clerk announces the entrance of the judge by saying, "All rise for the Honorable (insert the name), presiding."

3. The judge enters, sits the bench and says, "You may be seated."

4. The judge states the charge of the defendant (i.e., The Confederate States of America versus Elizabeth Van Lew, charged with spying).

5. The judge reads the stipulated facts. (This is a list of facts about the case that both attorneys agree upon. For example, Elizabeth Van Lew was a resident of Richmond, VA, in the Confederate States of America. She worked as a volunteer with wounded Confederate soldiers in a hospital in Richmond.)

6. The judge asks if each side is ready to begin, and each side says that they are ready.

7. The prosecuting attorney makes an opening statement summarizing how the people will prove that the defendant is guilty as charged. (In the case of Elizabeth Van Lew, as a citizen of the Confederate States of America, she is accused of betraying her country by spying for the United States.)

8. The defense attorney makes an opening statement and summarizes the defense's case, emphasizing that the burden of proof of the defendant's guilt is on the prosecution. (In the case of Elizabeth Van Lew, the defense points out that the prosecution has the burden to prove that she was actually a spy.)

9. The prosecution calls the first witness and conducts a direct examination.

10. The defense cross-examines the witness to try to weaken the witness' testimony.

11. Repeat the procedure for the second prosecution witness.

12. The defense calls the first witness and conducts a direct examination.

13. The prosecution cross-examines the witness.

14. Repeat the procedure for the second defense witness.

15. The prosecuting attorney presents a concluding argument emphasizing points that support the people's case.

16. The defense attorney presents concluding arguments.

17. The judge charges the jury with their duties.

18. The jury deliberates.

19. The jury returns a verdict. (If conditions are favorable, a jury member explains the reasons for the verdict.)

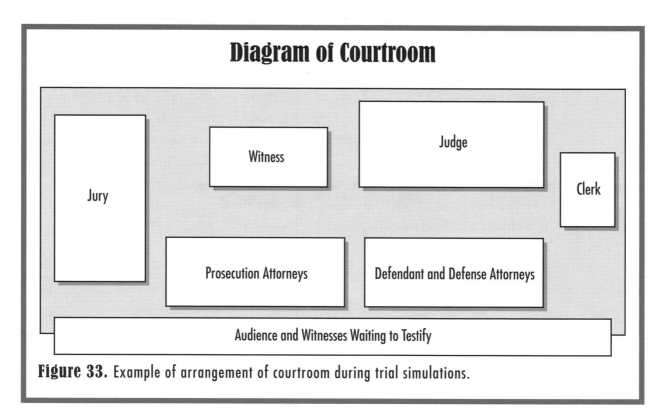

**Figure 33.** Example of arrangement of courtroom during trial simulations.

piece of physical evidence to the clerk who gives it to the witness, and objecting during opposing attorney's examination of a witness.

- *Physical evidence*: At the appropriate time during a witness' testimony, the examining attorney asks the judge's permission to introduce evidence. The judge will grant permission. The attorney introduces the evidence and names the evidence piece such as People's Exhibit A or Defense Exhibit A. Physical evidence includes items such as documents and objects in connection with witnesses' testimonies. (For example, during the prosecutor's examination of a wounded Confederate soldier, the prosecutor might ask the witness to identify a letter he had dictated to Elizabeth Van Lew to send to his mother. The letter would have referred to the place he had been fighting when he was wounded and mentioned that his unit would soon move from there to another specified location. The soldier would then read from the letter. Then the prosecution would call an officer of the Confederate army to the stand who would testify that when his troops arrived at that same specified location, Union troops were waiting for them in a trap.)

- *Occasions for objections*: If there are two attorneys to a side, the one to make objections is the one who examines the witness. The second attorney will give opening and closing statements. When raising an objection, the attorney should stand and address the judge saying, "Your honor, I object," or "Objection." The judge will ask for the grounds of the objection. After the objection is stated, the judge either overrules or accepts the objection and asks the jury to disregard the testimony that raised the objection, or asks the examining attorney to rephrase the question. Attorneys should be sparse with objections and only object with a truly valid possibility of the judge's acceptance.

- *Grounds for objections*: During a real trial, grounds for objections are complex and include many more objections than those listed here. In a virtual historical trial, it is necessary to scale objections to match the time frame and level of intricacy of the trial. Appropriate grounds for objection for a virtual historical trial include:
  - ▶ *Irrelevance*—The witness' testimony has no bearing on the case.
  - ▶ *Hearsay*—The attorney asks the witness to tell something that someone else has said.
  - ▶ *Opinion*—The witness is giving an opinion of what happened, not stating the facts of what happened. An example of an opinion: A wounded Confederate soldier whom Elizabeth Van Lew had visited in the hospital says, "I really think Mrs. Lew is a spy. She just has a sneaky way about her." Valid testimony would be, "I knew that Mrs. Lew did not mail the letter I had dictated to her because after she left, I looked out the window and saw her hand the letter to a man sitting on a park bench."
  - ▶ *Argumentative*—The attorney argues, harasses, or badgers the witness.

The following tips should help you direct students wanting to conduct a simulation of a historical trial.

1. The two sides of attorneys work together to set up their individual work. First, they agree on the stipulated facts of the case. These are basic facts that do not need to be established in witness testimony. Stating them at the beginning of the trial saves time and orients the jury to the case. In the case of Elizabeth Van Lew, both sides agree that she was a volunteer in a hospital for wounded Confederate soldiers. This does not mean that she used her position to gain information, but the defense cannot dispute that she worked at the hospital. Another fact is that the defendant was a Southerner. Second, identify witnesses. It is fair for each side to know who will testify. Attorneys do not have to disclose what their witnesses will say, but it gives the opposing side an opportunity to research what the witness probably will say. This gives the attorneys a chance to prepare for cross-examination.

2. The two sides of the attorneys then work separately to build their cases. They work with their own witnesses to bring out the strongest points for their case, and they develop their opening and closing arguments.

3. Remember that the attorneys, defendant, and witnesses need to be real people of the past. Attorneys will be the most difficult to identify because they might not have surfaced in your research. Try to find out who some of the lawyers were at the time of the trial; even they had nothing to do with the case in real life, you can pretend that they were part of the trial. Be sure to cast them in a role consistent with their work and try to associate them with the topic of the trial. Many historical figures who were noted for contributions other than practicing law were attorneys at significant trials. During colonial times, John Adams was the defense lawyer for the British soldiers in the Boston Massacre. He later became the second President of the United States. His son, John Quincy Adams, who also became President of the United States, defended the captives of the slave ship *Amistad* before the Supreme Court. It would therefore not be unusual for a famous person who was also a lawyer to appear in virtual trials.

4. Use the research gathered for the historical paper to bring out the personalities and character of attorneys and witnesses to add to the reality of the trial. Sometimes the attitudes and demeanor of these people makes a difference in how a jury relates to the case. For example, historical figures, like people of today, were actually quite arrogant, shy, eloquent, hostile, wise, sarcastic, gentle, and characterized by other unique traits.

5. The attorneys should identify themselves to the jury and tell why they are participating in the case. The jury will become acquainted with the defendant during the trial. They will come to know the witnesses because the attorneys will establish why they are qualified to give testimony, but the lawyers will need to identify themselves. If you use two prosecutors and two defense attorneys, the lawyer making the opening statement introduces his or her colleague.

6. Dressing in period clothing adds to the reality of the trial.

7. Check closely to see where the people of the trial were and what they were doing at the time of the trial. For example, the Confederate soldier testifying against Mrs. Lew might have been in the hospital, at home recovering from his wound, or back on the battlefield at the time the trial would have occurred. You need to establish all of the participants' locations and occupations to be certain that they would have been available to participate at the time of the trial.

8. After students have planned their case, ask a lawyer to volunteer his or her time to review the case with your students and advise them about how to

strengthen their case. Clarify courtroom procedures with the lawyer and ask any questions about matters of concern.

9. Have the students write thank you notes to the judge and the lawyers who helped them with their case.

## MEDIA PRESENTATIONS

Media presentations are exciting ways for students to communicate what they have learned from writing their historical papers. Media presentations afford students several options for constructing a video or DVD, computer presentation, or Web site. One choice is to visually recreate a historical paper using its contents as an outline. In this method, students can begin with the introduction to their papers, use images to support the premise, and insert the conclusion at the end of the presentation. For example, if a student creates a Web site, he or she could set up the premise of the paper through a brief text introduction from the historical paper. Then, the student could state the paper's points and link each point to Web sites that illustrate the points. The site could end with the historical paper's conclusion. Another option is to develop a single aspect of a historical paper. For example, if a student wrote about the spread of the bubonic plague in Europe in the 14th century, he or she might concentrate a media presentation on sanitary and medicinal practices of that time. Media presentations are discussed in more detail in the sections that follow. A rubric for evaluating media presentations is included in Figure 34.

One of the most effective tools for organizing the creation of a media presentation is the storyboard. Using a storyboard is a highly effective organizational tool because the technique allows students to mock up their presentation before creating it and then look at it as a whole. Once students have their storyboards in place, they can rearrange their scenes or slides for continuity and seamless flow from one segment of the presentation to the next. Blank templates for storyboarding videos or DVDs, computer presentations, and Web sites appear in Figures 35, 36, and 37.

The completed templates in Figures 38, 39, and 40 deal with the geographic and environmental changes in the land beyond the Missouri River from 1806 to the present time. This is the territory the Lewis and Clark Expedition covered from 1804–1806. You may want to make copies of the blank templates so that you will have plenty on hand when students begin the organization process.

Because students will probably not have hard copies of their images, they can use sticky notes to represent each image and refer to them by description such as "Native Americans meeting with Lewis and Clark," or "drawing of a fish in Clark's journal." For videos and DVDs, label sticky notes with segments such

| Rating | Historical Quality | Presentation Quality |
|---|---|---|
| 4 (highest level) | • Accurately represents the events and concepts of the historical paper.<br>• Strongly reflects the historical framework of the topic.<br>• Strongly reflects the historical significance of the topic. | • Settings and backgrounds contribute to the spirit of the content of the topic.<br>• Transitions are smooth and consistent with the subject matter.<br>• Presentation of content is appealing.<br>• Selections for presentation capture the spirit and theme of the topic.<br>• Grammar is correct and appropriate. |
| 3 | • Represents the events and concepts of the historical paper somewhat accurately.<br>• Somewhat reflects the historical framework of the topic.<br>• Somewhat reflects the historical significance of the topic. | • Settings and backgrounds adequately reflect the spirit of the content of the topic.<br>• Transitions are somewhat smooth and consistent with the subject matter.<br>• Presentation of content is interesting.<br>• Selections for presentation reflect the spirit and theme of the topic.<br>• Grammar is correct and appropriate. |
| 2 | • Represents the events and concepts of the historical paper with limited accuracy.<br>• Refers to the historical framework of the topic.<br>• Refers to the historical significance of the topic. | • Settings and backgrounds are occasionally appropriate to the topic.<br>• Transitions are random and occasionally smooth.<br>• Presentation of content is of adequate interest.<br>• Selections for presentation are limited in explaining the topic.<br>• Grammar is occasionally correct and appropriate. |
| 1 | • Haphazardly represents the events and concepts of the historical paper.<br>• Ignores or misrepresents the historical framework of the topic.<br>• Ignores or misrepresents the historical significance of the topic. | • Settings and backgrounds are haphazard in their relationship to the topic.<br>• Transitions are awkward.<br>• Presentation of content lacks interest.<br>• Selections for presentation are incomplete and sometimes irrelevant to the topic.<br>• Grammar is seldom correct and appropriate. |

**Figure 34.** Rubric for evaluating a visual project: Media presentations.

**Storyboard**

| Subject on film: | Background sound: |
| --- | --- |
| Action: | Voiceover: |

**Figure 35.** Blank storyboard template for creating videos and DVDs.

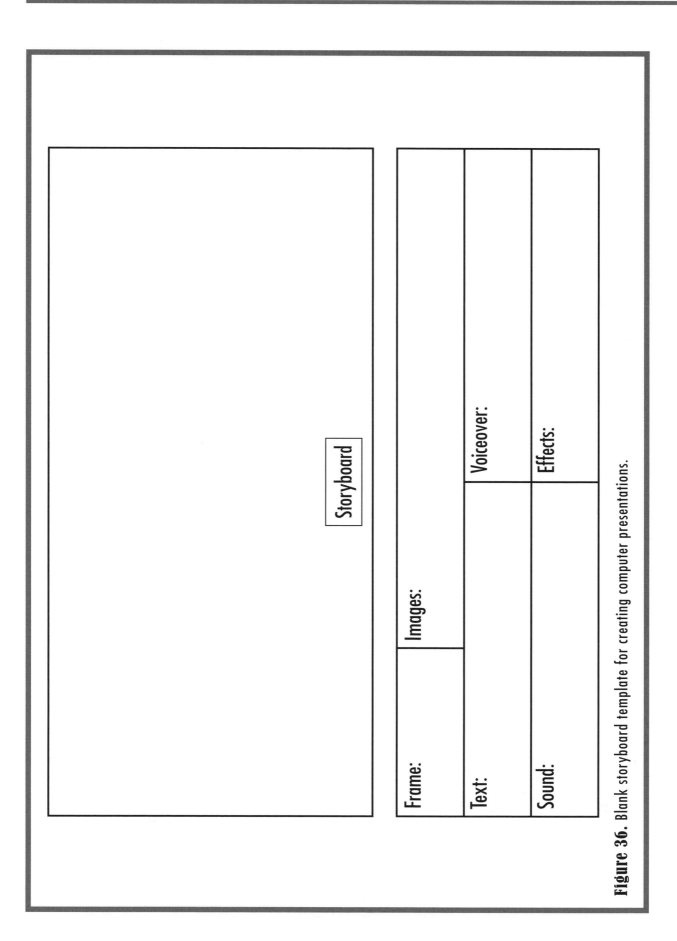

**Figure 36.** Blank storyboard template for creating computer presentations.

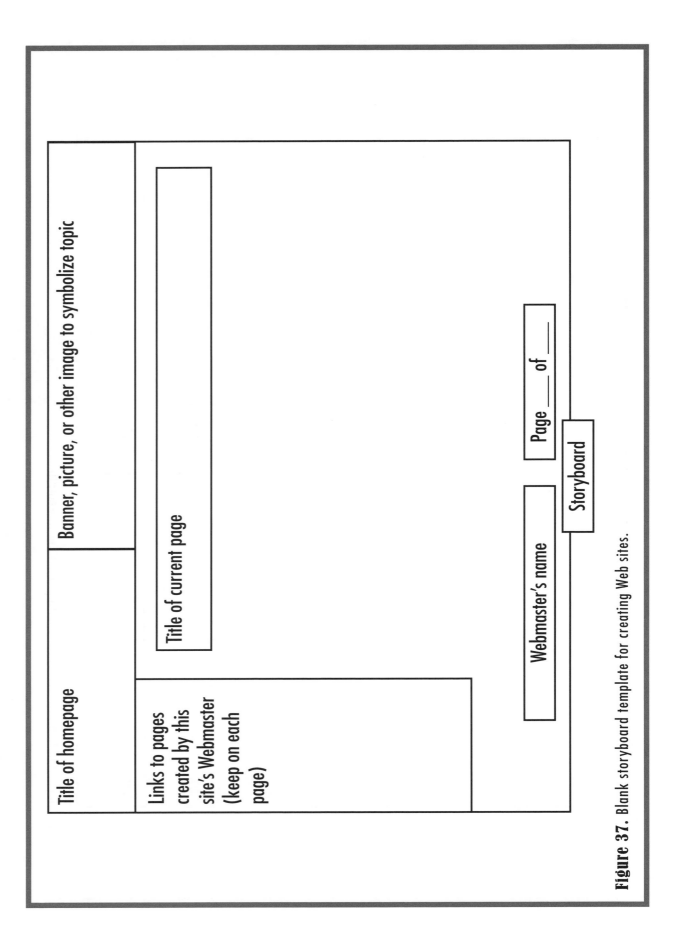

**Figure 37.** Blank storyboard template for creating Web sites.

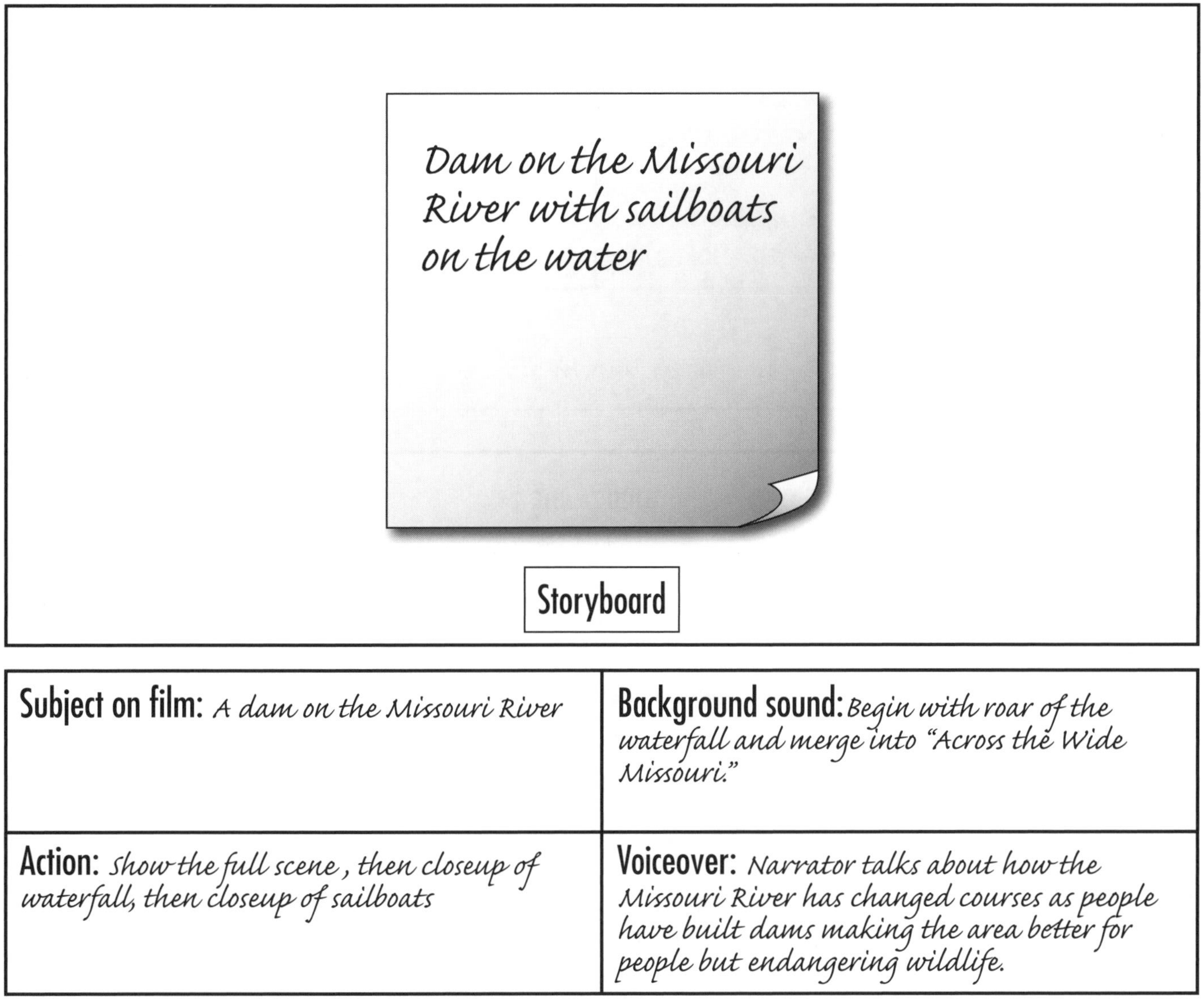

**Storyboard**

Dam on the Missouri River with sailboats on the water

**Subject on film:** A dam on the Missouri River

**Action:** Show the full scene, then closeup of waterfall, then closeup of sailboats

**Background sound:** Begin with roar of the waterfall and merge into "Across the Wide Missouri"

**Voiceover:** Narrator talks about how the Missouri River has changed courses as people have built dams making the area better for people but endangering wildlife.

**Figure 38.** Completed storyboard template for creating videos and DVDs.

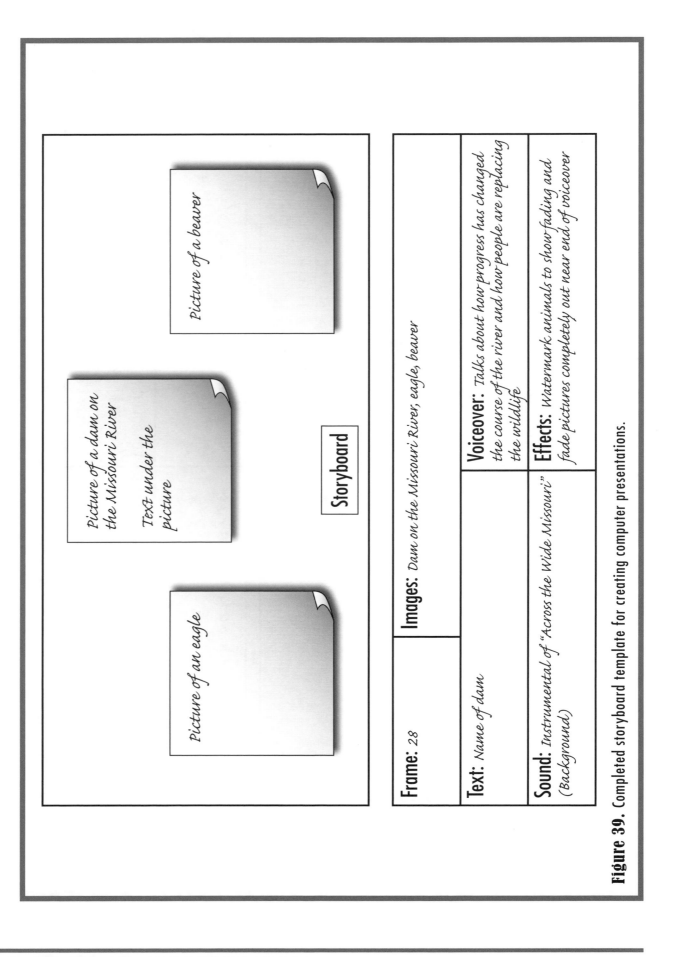

**Storyboard**

**Frame:** 28 | **Images:** *Dam on the Missouri River, eagle, beaver*

**Text:** *Name of dam*

**Voiceover:** *Talks about how progress has changed the course of the river and how people are replacing the wildlife*

**Sound:** *Instrumental of "Across the Wide Missouri" (Background)*

**Effects:** *Watermark animals to show fading and fade pictures completely out near end of voiceover*

*Picture of a dam on the Missouri River*

*Text under the picture*

*Picture of an eagle*

*Picture of a beaver*

**Figure 39.** Completed storyboard template for creating computer presentations.

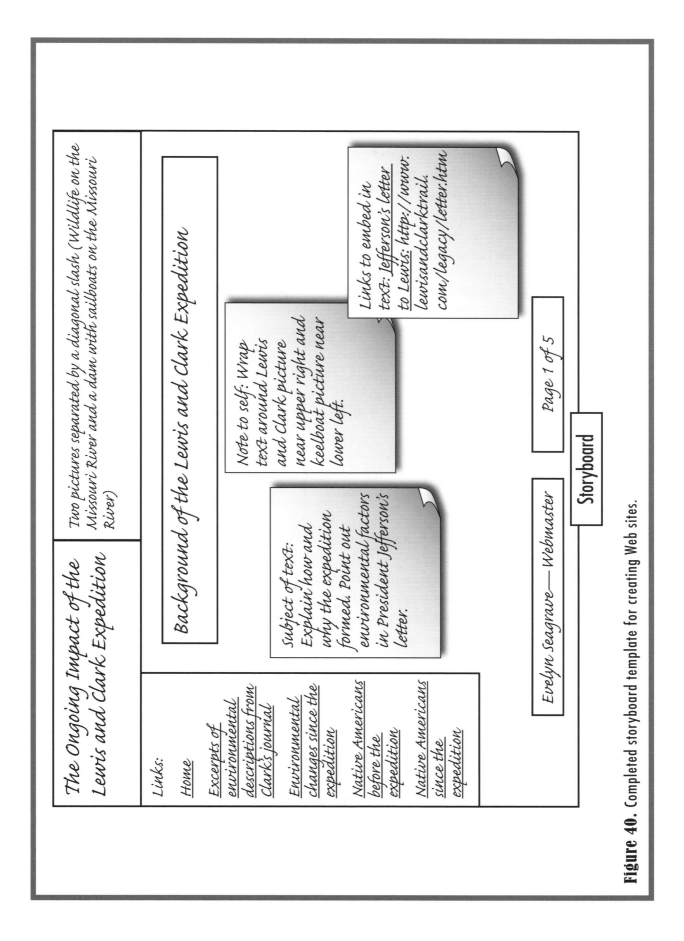

**Figure 40.** Completed storyboard template for creating Web sites.

as "interview with Dr. Bernal," or "film segment of flying eagles." Moviemakers usually draw their scenes on the storyboard so that they can visualize the flow of the action. If students want to use artwork, it does not have to be beautiful, just functional.

To use these templates, students should lay them on a table or tape them to a wall so that they can be easily viewed and reviewed side-by-side. Students will want to be able to either switch the pages around or switch the sticky notes from page to page as they put their action together. Once the flow of the presentation is established using the storyboard method, students can flesh out their text pieces and voiceover scripts, and then assemble the full presentation.

For additional ideas and tips for creating and using storyboards, check out the following Web sites:

- Acting with a Pencil: Storyboarding your Movie: http://www.exposure.co.uk/eejit/storybd
- Creating the Storyboard: http://www.uncc.edu/webcourse/sb/storyboard.htm
- Storyboarding "A Recipe": http://www.storycenter.org/memvoice/pages/tutorial_3.html
- *Twister* storyboards (From the movie *Twister*): http://movies.warnerbros.com/twister/cmp/storyboards.html

**Videos or DVDs**

Many students enjoy making videos and DVDs, both for the creativity they get to use in the process and for that feeling of expression such mediums provide. Some schools have video cameras on hand for students to use, or students may wish to use a camera provided by a parent or family member. If you include videos and DVDs in your options for visual projects, make sure that students who do not have access to this expensive equipment at home have a way to access the equipment at school (check with your librarian or media specialist to see what is available for students). You should also check into video or DVD creation software. The majority of today's computers come with the memory and capacity to handle video creation software. Some, like Apple's iBook and iMac, come with the video production software built-in (iMovie, in this case). Again, check with your media specialist, school librarian, or district technology representative to make sure that students who do not have access to this software at home have a chance to use it on the school grounds.

Some videos and DVDs will require students to interview witnesses or people surviving during a certain event or time period. Direct students to the section and tips on conducting interviews found in Chapter 4 to help them conduct this portion of their video professionally.

Other tips for creating videos include:

1. You might feel limited in gathering sufficient images, because you cannot go back in time and film historical events as they unfolded. To take viewers into the past, you can include interviews with people who are experts about their topic such as museum staff and university professors. If the topic concerns more recent events, students could video interviews with people who have experienced the event firsthand, such as a medic who served in Vietnam or a woman who maintained a victory garden during World War II.

2. Insert still images, such as documents, maps, and photographs with voiceovers and/or music to bring the stills to life. These kinds of images are important to help you tell a story, but you will want to spend only a small fragment of time showing still images.

3. Keep camera movements steady and to a minimum. Use a tripod when possible, but if it is necessary to hold the camera, keep it steady. Pan subjects as little as possible. Zoom in and out of subjects slowly. This helps viewers to accommodate the movement.

4. Be careful of the backgrounds used when filming. Make backgrounds simple and free from busy designs and objects that detract from the main subject. Watch the lighting. Bright light in the background can darken and obscure the subject.

## Computer Presentations

Creating computer presentations is an effective way to communicate understanding of historical events, issues, and concepts. Students can insert historical images, authentic music of given time period, and even excerpts of recorded speeches from historical figures. Appropriate use of text completes a quality presentation.

Some tips you might share with students to help them create computer presentations are listed below.

1. Make the historical framework and historical significance of the topic a highlight of the presentation. Blend text and images in a way that sets up the premise of the historical paper and supports the main idea.

2. Be consistent with the background and animation. These are secondary elements, so they should not distract your viewers.

3. Use a variety of images and sounds. Incorporate music and voiceovers when appropriate.

4. When possible, use primary material to capture the reality of the time period. For example, if your topic is about the inventions of Thomas Edison, you might want to show a picture of a phonograph with background music of the period such as "Alexander's Ragtime Band."

5. Be certain that the presentation is self-explanatory. It will be helpful if students are available at the close of their presentations to answer questions and elaborate on their topic if viewers are interested. However, the presentation itself should communicate clearly and fluidly without a need for comments or explanations as it runs.
6. Use correct grammar, spelling, and punctuation in all text items.

## Web Sites

This medium is an ideal opportunity for students who enjoy constructing Web sites to make a useful contribution to people searching for information about a historical topic. It is exciting for students to realize that people of all ages and in all parts of the world are actually using their creation. You might want to stress that sharing understanding in this way requires work of exceptional quality.

The following are tips for creating an effective Web site:

1. Keep in mind that the Web site will be posted on the World Wide Web and therefore will have a vast audience and a lasting product. This is an exciting prospect, but also one of great responsibility to make your work useful to those who access your site.
2. Reflect the historical paper accurately and as fully as possible. You might want to write out your introduction, or maybe just your premise statement, because supplying background information for your topic will be useful to your viewers.
3. Use text sparingly, but effectively. Most people browsing the Internet are drawn to visuals. Interspersing your text with images brings your message to life. You might use thumbnails on your main page and provide enlarged pictures with a click on the images.
4. Be considerate of your users, and remember that your goal is to communicate. Avoid using devices that people have to access to view your site. Many of your viewers will be students using school computers, and they will be unable to add software. Also, some people have Internet servers that load slowly, so they will be unwilling to wait for an animation to appear. You can enhance your page and make it attractive with color and layout design without including cumbersome effects.
5. Be selective with your links. Analyze them thoroughly before you decide to add in a link. Some considerations about links include:
   - Be certain that the link is on target and consistent with your topic. Some Web sites are extremely slanted and biased to the point that the declarations on the site are untrustworthy. It is best to use reliable sites such as the World Fact Book, the National Park Service, sites of historical events and historic places, museum sites, and established

organizations' sites such as the United Nations and the Library of Congress.

- Link to sites that go straight to your topic. Occasionally, a site will have a sentence or two about a certain topic buried deep inside the Web site. Searching for pertinent information can be tedious and even fruitless for your viewers.

- Link to sites that are friendly to use and read. Usually a site with only fine print text is too much to digest, but if it accurately and effectively presents your topic, you might want to use it sparingly. Avoid using sites that are too technical or too elementary. Your viewers might not have the background to absorb material filled with language and concepts that are overwhelming to them. Also, if the material is too basic, the viewer will not gain new knowledge and feel that the effort has been a waste of time.

- Examine all of a link's material and its links' material, as well. Avoid using links that contain matter that is irreverent, irrelevant, or inappropriate.

Creating visual projects is a fun and fulfilling way for students to learn about history and to communicate their understanding to others. An advantage of offering students a wide variety of projects to create is that students have an opportunity to work at their most productive level, and they have a chance to use their personal creative talents to express their knowledge and understanding of historical content. To be certain that students have done their best work, it is beneficial to build in times of reflection and analysis of their progress so that they can polish and refine their products.

# Refining Visual Projects

As your students advance in their work, encourage them to take time to review their rubrics and the checklist in the pocket of their journals. Instruct students to determine if they have sufficiently addressed each of the items on these lists in a high-quality manner.

Getting feedback from others is another productive way for students to refine their work. Often fresh eyes see something that a project creator might have overlooked. Students working in a group could analyze each other's work and give constructive suggestions for improvement. If students think this feedback is applicable, they can incorporate it into their work. Students who are working alone might want to get together with someone else who is working alone. They could examine each other's work and give constructive feedback.

Students can use the rubrics included in this chapter to help them analyze the work of others.

Refining and polishing products is vital for both historical papers and visual projects. By setting aside class time for this activity, students can understand the necessity of continually analyzing their work as they strive for excellence.

# Presenting Student Projects

After all of your students' hard work is complete, the time will finally come when they present their visual projects at a history fair or festival. This is a truly exciting time for you and your students. Remind students that once they are set up in their stations, they are on their own, so they need to be prepared. If circumstances make it appropriate for students to be available to talk to visitors, they need to be ready to discuss their work from the depth of knowledge and understanding they gained from researching and writing their historical papers. Depending on the purpose and venue of your fair or festival, you might require your students to give a brief oral presentation about their work. Encourage them to practice their delivery and be certain they present the core and heart of their topic's historical framework and historical significance as they discuss their work with visitors.

Help students realize that the presentation of themselves is as important as the presentation of their projects. Dressing and behaving appropriately at the history event demonstrates their respect for their visitors and for the people who work hard to make the event possible for them. This is an opportunity for students to think of themselves as professional historians who are sharing their expertise with an audience eager to know about their findings.

Participating in CATCH and displaying visual projects in a history fair or festival can be a momentous highlight of your students' school year. Each student will have accomplished researching and writing a historical paper like a true historian and each will have created a visual project like a professional. With your help, they will also have fun and learn in ways that will help them in their pursuit of knowledge and understanding all of their lives. Chapter 7 includes a detailed discussion of how teachers and parents can organize history fairs and festivals in their own schools and communities.

# Organizing a History Fair or Festival

The final stage in the CATCH process is organizing and conducting your history fair or festival. As you make plans for this event, you will want to analyze all of the necessary arrangement considerations including administrative issues, the magnitude of the event, and contest details. You may also consider having your students participate in a preorganized event such as the National History Day competition.

## Administrative Issues

As you formulate your plans for a history fair or festival to display your students' visual projects, you will need to confer with your principal. Most of these kind of public undertakings require expenses and arrangements for time and space. Your principal will let you know if there are budget allowances in place for you to use. You also will want to weigh the advantages of using school facilities versus community facilities for your history fair. If your plans are fairly involved, you will need to form a committee made up of other teachers, an administrator, parents, and perhaps people of the community to assist you in your efforts. Chapter 8 provides some tips and a letter for soliciting parent support for organizing history projects, fairs, and festivals. Each of the sections below also includes tips for handling some of the necessary administrative tasks that come with hosting such events.

## GRAND SCALE

| |
|---|
| *People involved:* All or most school students, faculty, staff, and administration; parents; community members; possibly other schools |
| *Time frame:* All day. |
| *Venue:* Total campus space or large community site |

## MODERATE SCALE

| |
|---|
| *People involved:* Many of the school students, faculty, staff, and administration; parents; community members |
| *Time frame:* Usually about 2–4 hours. |
| *Venue:* Part of the campus or a community site |

## SMALL SCALE

| |
|---|
| *People involved:* Students, teachers, parents, possibly some community members |
| *Time frame:* Usually short, 1–2 hours. Depends on if there is a connecting party. |
| *Venue:* Classroom, school commons, library, or cafeteria. Depends on if there is a connecting party. |

**Figure 41.** Magnitudes of history fairs and festivals.

# The Magnitude of Your History Fair

The extent of assistance you will need depends on the scale of your history fair. Three levels of involvement to consider as you formulate your plans for history fairs include grand scale, moderate scale, and small scale. Figure 41 shows a visual representation of the different magnitudes of history fairs.

## GRAND-SCALE EVENTS

Grand-scale history fairs are conducted over several hours and involve a large number of people affiliated with both the school and the community. This magnitude of history fairs includes all of your students and/or perhaps your whole grade or your entire school or district. Two examples presented here demonstrate two kinds of participation in a grand-scale event: an entire campus and only one teacher's students.

## Entire Campus Event

An example of an entire campus hosting a history festival is that held each year at Fannin Middle School in Amarillo, TX. Julie Greene, a librarian at the school, serves as director of the Fannin History Festival, organizing this event every October on the school campus. The festival combines displays of student-constructed historical models and historical demonstrations by people in the community and beyond. At this event, students have an opportunity to present their work and learn about history through hands-on experiences.

Greene says that the objectives of the festival are to reach out to the community; have fun with families, students, and teachers; and to raise money for field trips. Admission is $.50 for students and $1.00 for adults. Teachers also prepare and sell food at concession booths to raise extra money.

Fannin Middle school has 650 students in grades 6–8. Each student creates a model of a structure related to the curriculum, so sixth graders construct buildings in connection with world studies, such as the models of St. Isaac's Cathedral and the Spanish mission shown in Figure 29. Seventh graders depict significant structures in Texas history, and eighth graders build models of notable structures in American history.

With such a wide range in curricula, the festival spans a time period from early man to present day in both student and adult contributions. Julie secures presenters to show how people have lived across the centuries through crafts, demonstrations, reenactments, and storytelling (see Figure 42). Several Native Americans come from Oklahoma to erect teepees, dance, and tell legends. She also invites people to bring animals and explain their roles in mankind's historical development. These activities require the use of all areas of the campus including the library, two gyms, the commons area, the cafeteria, and the outside grounds, especially when you consider that in 2005, more than 2,000 people attended the history festival.

Such an enormous project definitely requires a lot of assistance for Greene. Everyone pitches in, including teachers, students, community organizations, and former students who enjoy coming back on campus as "tugger luggers" to haul around all the models on display and the equipment necessary for use in the event.

The contest portion of the festival takes place the day before the public event. Students show the products they have constructed according to a rubric designed by their teachers. They also write a paper about their models and give an oral presentation to their classmates. Teachers judge the models and award ribbons to the winners. When the visitors come to the festival the next

**Figure 42.** Viola Moore shows Michael Byrd how his ancestors prepared their food in pioneer days at the grand-scale history festival at Fannin Middle School in Amarillo, TX. Photo used with permission by Julie Greene.

day, they can view all of the projects and see which models received awards (J. Greene, personal communication, August 11, 2006).

For Julie Greene's tips on conducting a history festival on a grand scale, see Table 9. Although Greene's account offers details specific to her school, her ideas are helpful for others who plan to conduct a grand-scale history event.

## One Teacher's Event

An example of a grand-scale history event conducted by a single teacher is called "A Presidential Commemoration," and it works especially well for a teacher who has a number of American history classes. This model would also be suitable for several American history teachers working together. Although the presentation in this example is about American Presidents, it would serve for any topic having various components for representation such as "European Colonization of Africa" or "Cultural Developments of Southeast Asia."

This kind of event gives students an opportunity to share their knowledge and understanding with the community in a way that uses their special talents and abilities. It is also lets the community observe the academic aspects of a local school.

If possible, it is advantageous to hold the commemoration away from school so that the community will realize that the history fair is for everyone, not just parents and school personnel. The setting for this example is a shopping mall.

## Table 9
## Julie Greene's Tips for Hosting a Grand-Scale History Fair or Festival

- Set your date and stick to it so that your community will come to expect it when the time rolls around.

- Mine the gold in your community in the form of reenactors and people who demonstrate crafts (weaving, spinning, quilting), musicians, historical organizations and museums, archaeology societies, and animal handlers for horses, sheep, longhorn cattle, milk cows, and buffalo.

- Set up these people to conduct activities such as panning for gold (use pyrite), grinding corn, writing in calligraphy, using stone tools, creating petroglyph art, and making butter.

- Advertise.

  ▸ Have a flyer designed by a local advertising company, pro bono. Distribute to staff members, teachers, and elementary students in the district via the district mail system.

  ▸ Have your school's drama students visit each of your feeder schools to talk up the event. (Secure permission from principals and usage of buses. Plan to allow 4 days for this activity because students can only spend about one hour at each place.)

  ▸ Use the public service announcement system for local television and radio stations. On the morning of the event, arrange to have live radio coverage on site. This brings in a lot of people.

  ▸ Run a newspaper story the week before the event, including images of the previous festival. (Secure parental permission when showing children in the pictures.)

  ▸ Interview on early morning television and radio talk shows before the event.

- Make sure your logistics are covered.

  ▸ Order tables from district.

  ▸ Make sure electrical outlet are sufficient to carry the load of equipment using electricity.

  ▸ Hire off-duty policemen for security.

  ▸ Make sure air conditioning or heat is available for that day.

  ▸ Secure several sets of two-way radios for communication.

  ▸ Have a coffee and doughnut station set up for exhibitors the morning of the event.

## Table 9, Continued

- Teachers and students' concerns:

  ► Teaching teams each have a concession of food, drink, or candy to raise money for field trips.

  ► Students are assigned projects in their history classes, due the Friday before the event.

- Day of the event:

  ► Director comes in at 6 a.m. to set up registration table, coffee, and donuts.

  ► Tugger luggers (students) arrive at 7 a.m. to help exhibitors unload their cars, set up their stations, break down their stations at the close of the event, and reload their cars.

  ► Registration is from 7 to 9 a.m. The exhibitors and tugger luggers receive meal tickets for the concession stands.

  ► Gates open for the public at 9 a.m. and close at 3 p.m.

- On the Monday after the event, make notes about what worked well and what needs improvement for next year. Take care of any post-festival details, and send thank you e-mails to teachers and exhibitors. (J. Greene, personal communication, August 11, 2006)

The center of a shopping mall is an ideal location because people can attend the event while they take care of other matters. A mall is also spacious and can accommodate shoppers, as well as people who come just to attend the commemoration. Also, parking spaces are plentiful. A large community hall and other public facilities are also serviceable for this kind of fair.

Students involved in the commemoration write a historical paper and construct a visual project according to the CATCH approach. The topics and premises focus on any element of a president's or series of presidents' administrations. For example, a suitable topic could be the contributions of Eleanor Roosevelt as a First Lady or a comparison of how Jimmy Carter and Ronald Reagan treated Civil Rights issues. For an arrangement of possible stations, see the diagram in Figure 43. During the event, students work in shifts to display and discuss their projects.

Corresponding to the diagram in Figure 43, presentations could include:

1. *Speeches for nominating candidates for the Mt. Rushmore honor*: Students who wrote their historical papers about the impact and contributions of individual presidents might want to select this activity as their visual project. Use the following procedure:

    a. Post times for the event outside the area of presentation so that audiences can know when to gather to hear the speeches.

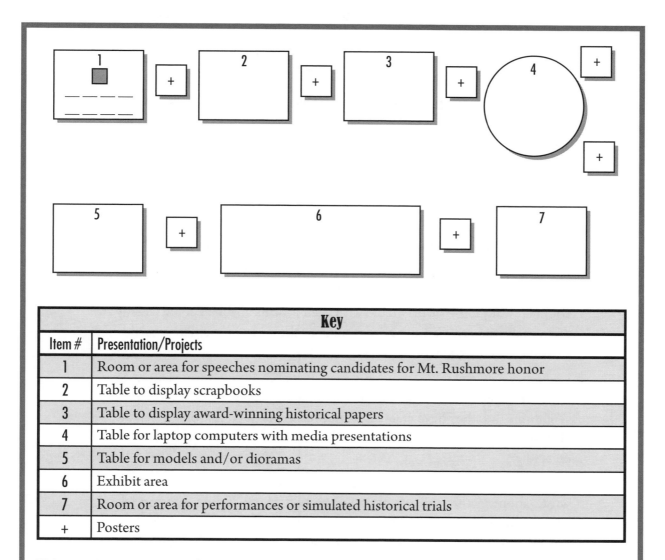

| Key | |
|---|---|
| **Item #** | **Presentation/Projects** |
| 1 | Room or area for speeches nominating candidates for Mt. Rushmore honor |
| 2 | Table to display scrapbooks |
| 3 | Table to display award-winning historical papers |
| 4 | Table for laptop computers with media presentations |
| 5 | Table for models and/or dioramas |
| 6 | Exhibit area |
| 7 | Room or area for performances or simulated historical trials |
| + | Posters |

**Figure 43.** Arrangement of presentations and projects at "A Presidential Commemoration" grand scale history event.

b. Have a master-of-ceremonies explain to the audience that they will hear three (probably no more than five) speeches from promoters of a certain president to be the new face on Mt. Rushmore. At the close of the final speech, the audience will vote on the president they believe deserves the honor based on the evidence presented in the speeches. George Washington, Thomas Jefferson, Abraham Lincoln, and Theodore Roosevelt are already carved into the mountain. (If your curriculum includes only the first or second half of American history, then students would nominate a president whose administration they will have studied during your course.)

c. Students give their speeches lasting no longer than 5 minutes. They can use supplemental materials such as posters, images, computer presentations, sound bytes from presidential speeches, and other audio or visual aids.

    d.   The master-of-ceremonies thanks the speakers and announces that it is time for the audience to vote by raising their hands when their choice of candidate is named.

    e.   Follow-up fanfare is optional.

2.  *Scrapbook display*: Some of the books might be about individual presidents or about a series of presidents who dealt with a common issue such as poverty, the economy, or foreign affairs. Students who created the scrapbooks stand by to explain and elaborate on their work to interested visitors.

3.  *Historical papers display*: Before the event, you or a designated judge may have given awards to students for their historical papers. The winners could appear on the display table with their awards visible. People usually do not take time to read an entire paper, but the authors could be available to discuss their work with visitors.

4.  *Multimedia presentations*: Students use laptop computers for visitors to either manipulate or watch as students operate videos or slideshow presentations that they have created about presidents. If conditions are favorable for Web access, students also can demonstrate any Web sites they have created.

5.  *Models and diorama display*: Students can draw on information they wrote about in their historical papers as they show and explain models and/or dioramas that include scenes such as the President's Oval Office, the Situation Room of the White House, or a scene depicting George Washington quelling the Whiskey Rebellion.

6.  *Exhibits*: These take up a large area because the display boards are large and supplementary materials might take up a lot of space. Therefore this part of the set-up would be permanent during the commemoration. However, students who have constructed their exhibits as a group can take turns manning their exhibits if they are unable to stay at the event all day.

7.  *Performances*: Post times for the event outside the area of presentation so that audiences can know when to gather to view the performances. These would include brief presentations such as monologues, plays, or reenactments. After the presentations, students could be available to answer questions from visitors and to discuss their historical papers to give more in-depth information about their performances. You might want to alternate these presentations with virtual historical trials, or if there is an abundance of performance entries, arrange with the mall management for more space or a separate room for the trial(s).

8. *Posters*: Indicated by a plus (+) sign in Figure 43, posters are scattered among and between display stations. These visuals reflect the core of the historical paper, and the students who created the posters could be available to discuss them.

Back in class on the following Monday, give students time to discuss their Presidential Commemoration adventure. Most students will be amazed that they felt like experts as they informed the public about the United States Presidents. Also, evaluate the event with your committee and note what went well and what needed improvement. Discuss the possibilities of conducting another grand-scale event next year.

## Other Logistics of Grand-Scale Events

If you choose to conduct a history fair of this magnitude, you will need a lot of assistance organizing and carrying out the event. A committee comprised of school and community volunteers will greatly facilitate the challenge. You should ask school employees from several different capacities to serve on the committee; the history faculty is, of course, always a good choice, but other key members of the school staff might also play a significant role. For instance, the drama or speech teacher might serve as an excellent organizer for the performance category of the event, the gym coach might be willing to supervise the set-up crew, the cafeteria manager could coordinate the morning coffee station and arrangement of food booths, and the school secretary could be an efficient and impartial organizer for the competition portion of the event. Other staff members with history backgrounds (such as principals, counselors, superintendents, and even school board members) could serve on the judging panel along with community members. Parents do not necessarily need a background in history to be willing, enthusiastic, and invaluable members of your planning committee. Some parents have a natural gift for organizing large-scale events and may prove invaluable to you as you attempt to coordinate the event during the out-of-school hours. Others can provide assistance with coordinating the set-up and use of laptops, making signs for each entry and student, registering students, contributing sack lunches, advertising via word of mouth or in businesses, and finding additional volunteers. Give each member of your committee a copy of the checklist in Figure 44. You may want to divide up the responsibilities on this checklist early in the planning stage.

One of the main considerations for a history fair that lasts all day is making arrangements for meals. You probably will want to set up a break area for volunteers with offerings of coffee and pastries. Lunch is a more complicated matter. If your budget allows, you might cater a sandwich meal for volunteers. Students could buy meals at food booths or at the mall food court. However,

| Completed | Tasks | Who Does It |
|---|---|---|
| | Designate a history fair coordinator. | |
| | Set up the budget for the history fair and assign someone to act as treasurer and pay bills. | |
| | Secure a place to conduct the history fair. | |
| | Arrange for use of all needed areas of the facility: parking, utilities, rooms, and hallways. | |
| | Coordinate volunteers: enlisting, assigning duties, and serving as their contact. | |
| | Coordinate judges: enlisting, contacting, and orienting them to their responsibilities the day of the fair. | |
| | Number and catalogue all project entries. | |
| | Create signs designating event areas and signs identifying each entry by student's name and entry title and number. | |
| | Affix signs in proper places prior to the event. | |
| | Publicize the fair and arrange for local media to attend and present a news story about it. | |
| | Create, print, and distribute schedules, programs, and name badges. | |
| | Determine prizes and awards and make arrangements for ordering, receiving, and awarding them. | |
| | Coordinate people for reception and information table. | |
| | Arrange for securing and setting up display tables, chairs, and podiums where needed. | |
| | Arrange for securing and setting up technical equipment: extension cords, microphones, and computer projectors. | |
| | Plan and carry out the awards ceremony. | |
| | Set up a break room for judges, volunteers, and staff to use during the fair. | |
| | Arrange for volunteers to receive and tally judges' sheets. | |
| | Create and distribute a schedule for students to bring their projects to the facility. | |
| | Create a schedule for students to be at their stations and/or make their presentations. | |
| | Purchase and arrange for food and coffee availability. | |
| | Clean the facility after its use and return all borrowed items. | |
| | Write thank you notes to volunteers and judges. | |

**Figure 44.** Checklist for preparing and conducting a grand-scale history fair with a contest.

you might be at a facility that does not have food booths or restaurants. Also, some students might not be able to afford to buy a meal. Several solutions to this matter would be workable. One is to schedule students to appear at the fair so that they will not be there the whole day and can eat before or after their time to present their projects. Another possibility is for students to bring a lunch, write their name on it, and deposit it for safe keeping in a designated location. Your school might provide tea and soft drinks for the students and other volunteers. Another possibility is for volunteers to make and deliver sandwiches, or an organization such as the PTA or PTO could cater a sandwich lunch for students and volunteers.

Additional tips regarding arrangements include:

1. It might be necessary to form subcommittees to facilitate all of the tasks involved in conducting a history fair. These groups could include parents, your principal or assistant principal, interested people from the community, and students.

2. Determine if the entries to the event will be judged. If so, you and your committee will need to decide on the awards and how winners will receive their awards. A subcommittee would secure judges and arrange a time for judging, either prior to or during the event. Perhaps the papers could be judged prior to the event and the remaining entries judged during the event.

3. Determine if expenses are necessary and if so, how the school will meet them.

4. Ask your principal to secure permission for using the facility hosting the event. You or someone from your committee will need to visit with the manager to work out all of the details.

5. Tasks for volunteers include:
   - Publicity, including pre-event advertising and arranging for a newspaper reporter and photographer to cover the event.
   - If entries are judged, secure judges and facilitate their means of judging.
   - If entries are judged, secure awards such as ribbons or trophies.
   - Secure and set-up tables and other necessary equipment for displays. If possible, supply chairs for audiences in the performance areas.
   - Arrange for electrical connections for computers and supplementary technical devices as they are needed in the display and performance areas.
   - Arrange for the loan of technical equipment such as computers, computer projectors, screens, microphones, and CD players.
   - Arrange with facility personnel the exact locations of the display areas including possible separate rooms for the speeches, performances, and virtual historical trials.

- Compose and distribute a set-up and presentation schedule to all involved personnel including teachers, students, and volunteers.
- Enlist two volunteers to assist at each display area during the event.
- Enlist several adults to be available in an overall capacity during the event.
- Enlist volunteers to help set-up prior to the event.
- Enlist volunteers to help dismantle stations after the event.
- Make signs labeling each of the display areas and signs announcing the times of the speeches and performances.
- Enlist volunteers to return all borrowed items.
- Write thank you notes to facility personnel, judges, and volunteers.

Scheduling of the event should be planned as far in advance as possible, especially if the event is to be held on school grounds. Organizers will want to check the district schedule, along with sports schedules, to make sure that no other events are already planned during that day in the campus areas in which you wish to hold the event. Sports events already planned for that day could draw in more visitors to the festival, but they can also keep students who wish to participate in the festival from being able to take part.

Other tips regarding scheduling include:
1. Saturday is usually the best day for this kind of event.
2. It is advisable for students and adults to set-up for the event between 7 and 8:45 a.m.
3. A suitable time for conducting the event is 9 a.m.–3 p.m.
4. If you have multiple classes, you might want to designate the first hour for your first period class, the second hour for your next period class, and so forth. However, if you are sharing the event with one or more teachers, you will need to work together to set up a schedule. If you have many students involved, you will want to rotate their time of presentation.
5. Allow time for quickly changing items from the scrapbook, historical papers, and models tables as the next shift of students arranges new items for display. If possible, leave the computers in place. However, if students use their own computers rather than those belonging to the school, they will want to take their computers with them when their shifts are over. Disconnecting one computer and connecting another one is a quick operation.
6. Schedule at least two adults to take turns manning each station to guard against theft and to be available for any problems that might arise.
7. If an awards ceremony is part of your plan, schedule it soon after the event concludes.

## MODERATE-SCALE EVENT

The primary differences between holding history events on a grand scale and on a moderate scale are the length of time of the event and the level of involvement of people organizing and conducting the event. Often a moderate-scale event takes place during a campus parents' night or one evening set aside for displaying a grade level's visual projects. These events usually last about 2 hours.

An example of a moderate-scale history fair is one conducted by the teachers, staff, and the 163 students of Kenedy Middle School in Kenedy, TX. Each March, they have an All American History Fair in connection with Texas Independence Day and Public School Week. The students' projects are directly tied to the Texas social studies standards (found in the state standards called TEKS) and to the state test. The teachers post the objectives from these documents on the school walls for parents to view when they attend the fair.

Social studies teachers Donna Patton, Lanny Hallmark, and Jan Jendrzey organize the 2-hour event, implementing details that result in a highly successful evening. These teachers also arrange funding for food served at the history fair's dinner through the PTO, and they secure door prizes for the guests, as well as awards for winners of the best essays and posters in grades 6, 7, and 8 from businesses in the community. The teachers personally provide materials used in decorations and other items, while the school supplies such items as paper to make placemats for the dinner and programs for the event.

Students participate in language arts classes by writing an essay about a topic associated with the United States in keeping with their grade-level curriculum. Therefore, sixth graders write about geographical features and influences of a state, seventh graders write about a significant impact of a person in Texas history, and eighth graders write about a significant impact of a person in early American history (in Texas, eighth graders study American history from 1607–1877; the remaining American history course is taught in high school).

In social studies classes, students construct a poster about their paper's topic. During the history fair, seventh- and eighth-grade students wear costumes that depict their historical figures. Sixth-grade students wear costumes representing people from the states they wrote about (D. Patton, personal communication, September 11, 2006).

To assist students in successfully accomplishing these assignments, the teachers provide detailed instructions and rubrics for the essays and posters. The teachers and staff of Kenedy Middle School make meticulous preparations to ensure a successful history fair. Well in advance of the fair, the teachers and staff meet regularly to discuss logistics and volunteer for necessary tasks. For a comprehensive list of their preparations, schedules, and activities, see Table 10.

# Table 10
# Arrangements for the Kenedy Middle School American History Fair

## Preliminary Matters

1. Send an invitation to parents to attend a dinner theater and the history fair.

2. Invite teachers and staff to dress as a famous American during the fair.

3. Designate custodial duties for the staff.

4. Secure someone to take photographs during the event.

5. Write an article for the local newspaper to appear prior to and after the event.

6. Secure judges for the essay and poster contests.

7. Prepare judging sheets.

8. Prepare nametags.

9. Secure awards for winners of the essay and poster contests.

10. Purchase food for the dinner including hot dog fixings, potato chips, and drinks.

11. Secure parent volunteers to contribute apple pies for the event.

12. Receive and store apple pies contributed by parents for the dinner.

13. Designate staff to greet the parents.

14. Prepare registration table and sign-in sheets.

15. Secure door prizes from community businesses and/or organizations.

16. Secure tickets with stubs for awarding door prizes.

17. Decorate the cafeteria and hallways.

18. Determine who will set-up, serve, and clean up after the dinner.

19. Assign all duties to be conducted during the history fair, including who will award prizes, supply music, and shake hands with parents as they leave the fair.

20. Set up poster displays in the hallways after school the day of the fair.

21. Write thank you notes to judges and parents who contributed the apple pies.

## Schedule for the History Fair (From 6–8 p.m.)

1. Before the parents arrive (5–5:45 p.m.):

   a. Set up tables and chairs as needed in the cafeteria and hallway.

   b. Set the United States and Texas flags in place on the stage.

   c. Be certain that all decorations are in place.

> d.  Photograph the posters, decorations, and decorated cake before the event, and people participating in activities during the event.
>
> e.  Greet and prepare judges.
>
> 2.  During the history fair:
>
>     a.  Greet and direct parents to the registration table.
>
>     b.  Begin serving the visitors dinner at 6 p.m.
>
>     c.  After dinner, the audience says the pledges of allegiance to the American and Texas flags and sings the National Anthem.
>
>     d.  The theater class presents a short American Civil War play.
>
>     e.  The principal invites the visitors to tour the three hallways to view the students' posters.
>
>     f.  At 7:15 p.m., the principal notifies everyone to gather in the cafeteria.
>
>     g.  The essay contest and poster winners receive awards.
>
>     h.  The principal draws ticket stubs and awards door prizes.
>
>     i.  The principal thanks everyone for coming and dismisses the visitors.
>
>     j.  The coaches stand at the doors and shake hands with parents as they leave.
>
>     k.  Teachers and staff help put away the tables and chairs and help store the leftover food.

The teachers and staff at Kenedy Middle School have found a way to use a history event to enhance parental involvement on their campus and to promote pride of accomplishment in their students. They also give students the opportunity to create visual projects based on their research and writing.

Many of the same tips for running a grand-scale event apply to those on the moderate scale, such as securing committee members and seeking out parent volunteers. Coordinators may want to go over the suggested checklist in Figure 44 and eliminate any tasks that do not apply to their particular fair. However, many teachers will find that most of the arrangement and scheduling logistics still apply to moderate-scale events, just on a smaller level.

## SMALL-SCALE EVENTS

Arranging and conducting a history event on any level is an involved process that requires a commitment to organizational efforts and a great deal of time. Occasionally, it is helpful to share this undertaking with another group. To conduct a history event on a small scale, connect with a group that conducts an annual affair already established in your community.

For example, some communities have festivals to commemorate the founding of the city, and many counties have fairs that last a week for judging farm animals. Museums and historical societies also sponsor fairs and festivals. Many of these events have booths and display areas for various purposes. Perhaps you could begin by having students' visual projects on display at your school in classrooms, libraries, and/or commons areas. Then you could select from these to display as part of the exhibits at a community event.

Your selections for public display could come from a contest at your school. If you are unable to use school time, you could submit your five best historical papers to a committee, historical society, or group of history professors to judge your students' work. You could also arrange for judges to meet you after school and tour the visual projects on display at your campus. The winning projects could then be on display at the community event.

## Adding a Contest Dimension to Your History Fair

If all or part of your history fair includes a contest, you will need to make provisions for this part of your event. It will be necessary to consult with your principal to determine the budget for prizes and awards. You might discover that you will need to ask community businesses and organizations to help bear the expense. If you order trophies or ribbons, you will want to do this well in advance of the history fair to assure that these items will be in place when you award them.

Securing judges for contests is a major undertaking and should be approached with great care and consideration. The judges need to be knowledgeable about the subject matter and recognize certain qualities of historical papers and visual projects such as historical accuracy, historical framework, and historical significance of the historical events and topics your students have presented. Professors and members of historical organizations usually enjoy serving as judges in this kind of special occasion. Many do not mind traveling up to 100 or so miles to participate in history fairs. If they do so, it might be necessary to pay their travel expenses, but most people will gladly do this without charge. It is a significant opportunity for them to apply and share their knowledge and expertise, so do not be reluctant to ask them to serve as judges.

Be sure to give judges considerations that will well equip them for their tasks. You might compile a packet for them and give them the materials 2 or 3 weeks ahead of the event. Each judge should be sent a letter along with the packet explaining your expectations (see Figure 45). Note that the letter includes an explanation of the historical framework and historical significance the students have been working from. It also includes information about

Dear Dr. Heflin,

Thank you for agreeing to serve as a judge in our upcoming history fair to be held at the Community Coliseum on May 12. Our students look forward to benefiting from your expertise.

To assist you in your preparation for our event, I am enclosing a schedule of the history fair, a copy of your judge's sheet, a list of titles and topics of the projects you will judge, a list of guidelines students used to create their products, and a rubric used to evaluate student's products in the classroom.

The category of entries you will be judging is exhibits. You will notice on the judge's sheet that students are responsible for demonstrating their topics' historical framework and historical significance. In this context, historical framework refers to the ideas and values of the people during the time period and in the setting of their topic. It also includes any relevant descriptions of geographic, social, and cultural influences regarding their topics. Historical significance refers to how the events and/or people have made a difference over time or how the issues involved are still under discussion and of concern today.

When you arrive at the coliseum, please park in Section 1A reserved for judges and volunteers. As you enter the front door, stop at the reception desk to register and to receive your name badge. Please be available to meet in the volunteers' break room behind the reception desk at 9 a.m. for a brief judges' orientation meeting. At that time, you will receive copies of the judges' sheets for the specific exhibits you will examine and a diagram of the location of the entries. Your judging duties will begin at 9:30 a.m. Students will be at their stations for interviews until 11 a.m. Please feel free to take your time in examining the exhibits and in visiting with students. When your judging is complete, please turn in your judges' sheets to the fair's secretary, Melanie Morrison, in the break room.

We invite you to enjoy coffee and pastries in the break room anytime during the day and to join us for a sandwich lunch in the break room any time between 11:30 a.m. and 1:30 p.m.

If you have any questions or concerns between now and the history fair, please contact me at jharrelson@yourschooldistrict.net.

Thank you for the valuable contribution of your time and expertise to our students.

Sincerely,

Juanita Harrelson
Colson ISD History Fair Coordinator

**Figure 45.** Sample letter to send to judges.

logistics that concern judges such as contacts, times, locations, parking, and food. The letter also refers to the enclosures in the packet.

The packet could include a copy of the rubrics for the historical paper and/or visual project, a copy of the tips for students that serve as guidelines in creating their work, a list of project topics and titles they will be judging, and a copy of the judge's sheet they will complete and return to you or whoever is assigned to interface with the judges. Examples of scoring sheets are included in Figures 46–53. You should make plenty of copies of these sheets (or of your own self-created scoring sheet) to have on hand for the judges on the day of the event. Students should receive a copy of the sheet pertaining to their project ahead of time, so that they can make adjustments and check to ensure that their project meets the judging requirements before the contest begins. In addition, you may want to give photocopies of the judges' comments to the students a few days after the event is completed. If you plan on doing this, ask the judges to write constructive comments on the sheets—comments that directly relate to the rubrics, historical framework and significance, and requirements of the student. Such constructive criticism is useful to help students learn what they can do differently the next year.

Other contest considerations concern logistics. It is important to set aside a specific time for the judges to be with the students and their projects. The category of the projects determines if viewers would be present at the same time judges are observing the entries. Judges can review historical papers apart from and before the history fair. If the category of a visual project is a performance or a media presentation, it is appropriate for judges to share that time with an audience. In the media categories, it is important for the judges to operate the computer presentation and browse the Web sites in order to determine the level of workability of the program they are judging. After the presentation, judges can interview students to gain a more complete idea of their depth of understanding about their topic.

Judges can observe exhibits, scrapbooks, posters, models, and dioramas before or during the history fair. It is important for students to be available for judges to interview them, so students would need to be notified in advance of when they need to be at their stations. If you decide for judges to do their work during the fair, you can either have them make their observations and student interviews while visitors are milling about, or you can shut down the exhibit area for an hour and allow only judges and students in that space during that time.

However you choose to arrange the judging procedures, it is important to have the judging early enough to determine the winners in time to set up for an awards ceremony. You should make sure to have a well-organized, responsible, and impartial adult in place to collect the sheets, tally them, and determine the winners. Because the sheets ask for the contestants' entry number instead of his or her name (or the groups' names), this person will be responsible for coordinating with the volunteer who labels each entry with a number to make sure that the correct contestants are awarded their prizes for their entries.

Another consideration is how to judge only one or two entries in a category. If you have given students many categories to choose from, some of the categories might only have a few entrants. The simulated historical trial and Web site option are examples of categories that might not draw many students. In the case of the trial, students can receive awards on the basis of scoring. For example, in a trial, the prosecution team might score higher than the defense team. In categories where group efforts cannot be easily broken down by their contributions, students can receive awards according to their team score. For example, a score between 95 and 100 might receive a blue ribbon while a score between 90 and 94 might receive a red ribbon. This system can also apply for an individual in a category without competition.

A category does not automatically have a winning student or group of students. If the judges do not believe that a paper or project category has an entry of quality caliber, then no one would receive an award for it. All of the judges' sheets have a maximum score of 100. You would probably only want to provide awards to students with a score of 80 or above.

To add a deeper dimension to your history fair, you might want to invite clubs and organizations to present prizes at the awards ceremony. These groups would be responsible for making their own judgments and securing their own awards, which could range from plaques, to books, to money. The local chapter of the Daughters of the American Revolution might give an award for the best historical paper about a Revolutionary War heroine, the county historical society might award the best visual project about a local historical event, or the Rotary Club might award a student for the best project about a historical figure who contributed a humanitarian service. This is an effective way to draw in the community and to recognize students who created worthy projects, but might not have placed in the contest according to the judges' scoring sheets.

Whatever scale of history fair you may conduct or whether students enter a contest, using the CATCH approach to writing historical papers and creating visual projects that reflect those papers provides exciting and highly effective learning opportunities for students. Teachers who take part in this kind of experience feel that it is well worth the time and effort required to engage in this experience.

# Judge's Score Sheet for Historical Papers

Title _____ Entry # _____

Scoring Guide:   10 points = Excellent
                  5 points = Good
                  3 points = Fair

| Historical Quality: | Score |
|---|---|
| Presented the topic with historical accuracy. | |
| Captured the ideas and values of the people in the paper's topic. | |
| Captured the topic's geographical influences. | |
| Captured the relevance of the topic's cultural and social issues. | |
| Captured the historical significance of the paper's topic. | |
| Research Quality: | Score |
| Used secondary sources effectively. | |
| Used primary sources effectively. | |
| Annotated the bibliography effectively. | |
| Presentation Quality: | Score |
| Presented the premise, supporting points, and conclusion convincingly. | |
| Wrote with clarity and correct grammatical usage. | |
| Total Points | |

Comments:



Judge's Signature _____

**Figure 46.** Judges' score sheet for historical papers.

# Judge's Score Sheet for Virtual Historical Trials

Defendant _____ Charge _____ Entry # _____

Scoring Guide:    10 points = Excellent
                  5 points = Good
                  3 points = Fair

| | Prosecution | Defense |
|---|---|---|
| **Historical Quality** | Score | Score |
| Depicted historical accuracy. | | |
| Used believable and appropriate evidence for the historical circumstances of the case. | | |
| Reflected the historical circumstances of the charge during direct examinations. | | |
| Reflected the historical circumstances of the case during opening and closing statements. | | |
| Captured the historical significance of the circumstances of the case. | | |
| **Performance Quality** | Score | Score |
| Used evidence and testimony that captured the essence of the case. | | |
| Used logic in developing and presenting the case. | | |
| Applied skill in examining witnesses. | | |
| Witnesses showed knowledge and understanding appropriate for their roles. | | |
| Used proper courtroom procedures. | | |
| Total Points | | |

Comments:

Judge's Signature_____

**Figure 47.** Judge's score sheet for virtual historical trials.

# Judge's Score Sheet for Plays, Monologues, Storytelling, and Reenactments

Title of Presentation: _____ Entry # _____

Scoring Guide:  10 points = Excellent
5 points = Good
3 points = Fair

| Historical Quality | Score |
| --- | --- |
| Depicted historical accuracy. | |
| Captured the historical framework of the topic's period. | |
| Used dialogue appropriate for the people of the topic's time period and setting. | |
| Portrayed the people of the time period with authenticity. | |
| Used costumes, props, and/or sets consistent with the topic's time period and setting. | |
| Captured the topic's historical significance. | |
| **Presentation Quality** | **Score** |
| Delivered lines and movement efficiently. | |
| Kept in character of the people portrayed. | |
| Used appropriate demeanor and gestures. | |
| Used safe and reasonable props and sets. | |
| Total Points | |

Comments:



Judge's Signature_____

**Figure 48.** Judge's score sheet for plays, monologues, storytelling, and reenactments.

# Judge's Score Sheet for Speeches

Title of Speech: _____ Entry # _____

Scoring Guide:     10 points = Excellent
                          5 points = Good
                          3 points = Fair

| Historical Quality | Score |
|---|---|
| Depicted historical accuracy. | |
| Captured the essence of the speech's issue or concept. | |
| Captured the historical framework of the time period. | |
| Captured the historical significance of the speech's topic. | |
| *If the speech was informative:* Gave appropriate and meaningful information surrounding the historical concepts of the topic. | |
| *If the speech was persuasive:* Presented convincing and appropriate arguments for the time period and circumstances of the speech. | |
| **Presentation Quality** | **Score** |
| Demonstrated understanding of the speech's topic. | |
| Delivered the speech with confidence. | |
| Made appropriate eye contact with the audience. | |
| Used correct grammar. | |
| Spoke with clarity at an appropriate pace. | |

Total Points [ ]

Comments:




Judge's Signature_____

**Figure 49.** Judge's score sheet for speeches.

# Judge's Score Sheet for Exhibits, Scrapbooks, and Posters

Title of Work: _____ Entry # _____

Scoring Guide:    10 points = Excellent
                   5 points = Good
                   3 points = Fair

| Historical Quality | Score |
|---|---|
| Depicted historical accuracy. | |
| Captured the heart of the historical topic. | |
| Captured the historical framework of the period. | |
| Used images and text appropriate for the topic and the period. | |
| Captured the historical significance of the topic. | |
| **Presentation Quality** | **Score** |
| Aligned the design's components with the topic's concepts. | |
| Achieved a pleasing balance between images and text. | |
| Selected appropriate images and text for the topic's concepts. | |
| Application of components was neat and orderly. | |
| Used correct grammar in presentation of text. | |
| Total Points | |

Comments:

Judge's Signature _____

**Figure 50.** Judge's score sheet for exhibits, scrapbooks, and posters.

# Judge's Score Sheet for Models and Dioramas

Title of Work: _____ Entry # _____

Scoring Guide:   10 points = Excellent
               5 points = Good
               3 points = Fair

| Historical Quality | Score |
| --- | --- |
| Depicted historical accuracy. | |
| Captured the historical framework of the work's time period. | |
| Used supplementary enhancements and explanations consistent with the work's time period. | |
| Reflected the purpose of the structure or scene. | |
| Captured the historical significance of the work. | |
| **Presentation Quality** | **Score** |
| Adheres to an appropriate structural scale. | |
| Used materials consistent with materials the work represents. | |
| Reflected the purpose of the structure or scene. | |
| Constructed the work neatly and orderly. | |
| Used correct grammar in text of supplementary materials. | |
| Total Points | |

Comments:



Judge's Signature_____

**Figure 51.** Judge's score sheet for models and dioramas.

# Judge's Score Sheet for Videos, DVDs, and Computer Presentations

Title of Work: _____ Entry # _____

Scoring Guide:  10 points = Excellent
5 points = Good
3 points = Fair

| Historical Quality | Score |
|---|---|
| Depicted historical accuracy. | |
| Captured the historical framework of the time period and setting of the topic. | |
| Selected images that reflected the heart of the topic. | |
| Selected supplementary inserts such as music and text that reflected the heart of the topic. | |
| Captured the historical significance of the topic. | |
| **Presentation Quality** | **Score** |
| Balanced images and text effectively. | |
| Selected pleasing and uncluttered backgrounds. | |
| Effected seamless scene shifts. | |
| Presented clear and decipherable images. | |
| Used correct grammar. | |
| Total Points | |

Comments:

Judge's Signature _____

**Figure 52.** Judge's score sheet for videos, DVDs, and computer presentations.

# Judge's Score Sheet for Web Sites

Title of Work: _____ Entry # _____

Scoring Guide:    10 points = Excellent
                   5 points = Good
                   3 points = Fair

| Historical Quality | Score |
|---|---|
| Depicted historical accuracy. | |
| Captured the historical framework of the time period of the topic. | |
| Selected appropriate images for the time period and the topic. | |
| Linked to appropriate sites for the time period and the topic. | |
| Captured the historical significance of the topic. | |
| **Presentation Quality** | **Score** |
| Balanced images and text effectively. | |
| Implemented user-friendly techniques. | |
| Linked to appropriate sites that enhanced and clarified the topic. | |
| Linked to wholesome and scholarly sites. | |
| Used readable fonts and correct grammar. | |
| Total Points | |

Comments:




Judge's Signature_____

**Figure 53.** Judge's score sheet for Web sites.

**Figure 54.** Roshan Govindbhai paints a performance background in Luisa Castillo's history class. Photo used with permission by Luisa Castillo.

# National History Day Competitions

Chris Terrill, a middle school history teacher in Kansas, has her students participate in National History Day each year. National History Day is a nationwide organization that sponsors competitive history fairs. Following NHD rules and regulations, students create projects, enter them in local history fairs, and the winners advance to district, state, and national contests. This is a grand-scale event, so she and her students invest quite a bit of time in the program. Of the benefits of this endeavor, she says,

> The students get a chance to become experts. They know by the time they are done that very few people they come in contact with will have the knowledge of their topic they do. When they get this in depth, they get really excited about every tidbit of new knowledge they find. They like the creativity of putting their final product together. (C. Terrill, personal communication, November 19, 2004)

Luisa Castillo, a high school teacher in New Mexico, also has her students participate in National History Day. To keep close to her required curriculum, she gives the students choices of broad topics. The students then narrow their topics and proceed with their projects. Because the students are working on subjects they would learn during class time, Luisa is able to allow students to work on part of their projects during history class (see Figure 54).

Several of Luisa's students have participated in competitions and have been quite successful in their efforts. In the Spring of 2005, her students Jesús Hernández, José Mercado, and Hector Urquidi won first place in their regional and state history fairs. Then, at the National History Day competitions in June of that year, they were awarded the "Best of State" competition for their documentary about the Navajo Code Talkers in World War II. Figure 55 shows the three students hard at work on assembling their documentary before the

**Figure 55.** Jesús Hernández, José Mercado, and Hector Urquidi build and edit their award-winning documentary using computer software. Photo used with permission by Luisa Castillo.

competition phase. Luisa enjoys watching her students learn through working on these comprehensive projects. "It is most rewarding to see students go from an idea to a solid project that they can be really proud of," she said (L. Castillo, personal communication, June 23, 2005).

Students and teachers who wish to participate in National History Day competitions should seek information about the event from the organization's Web site: http://www.nationalhistoryday.org. Teachers should be sure to review and print out the rules for the competition before embarking on this process.

Whether your students are part of a contest or whether they participate in a CATCH history fair on a grand scale, a moderate scale, or a small scale, they will benefit from the learning opportunity of researching and writing a historical paper and of creating a visual project based on their topic. They will experience the accomplishment of thinking and producing like a historian.

# CHAPTER 8

# Getting Parents Involved

**C**ATCH is an ideal project for involving parents in your students' learning experiences and in your classroom activities. Students can benefit from parental assistance in researching their topics and in constructing their visual projects, and you can benefit from the volunteer services parents can provide. Many parents are also glad to have the opportunity to participate in an academic venture with their children. Once parents are engaged, they often get just as excited about the projects as their kids.

Although the role of parents is necessarily limited because students are responsible for their own work, parents still have contributive avenues of involvement. You can help them clarify their role by supplying them with a list of ways they can assist their children (see Table 11).

You also might want to send a letter to your students' parents explaining the CATCH approach, requesting their help with the history fair, and providing a means for them to volunteer their services. Figure 56 is a sample letter informing parents about the fair and asking them for their help. Figure 57 is a form for parents to complete to volunteer their services.

Parents are also valuable for providing supplies for classroom use (especially in donating items like construction paper for mounting photos, photo paper for printing photos, and props and costumes for performances). Keep in mind that some students' parents may not be able to afford to provide supplies, but might be willing to donate their time and effort on the day of the event or in the process of constructing projects. You should always keep on hand useful supplies for students whose parents cannot afford to provide them with supplies, including poster board, construction paper, typing paper, access to computers and the Internet, access to printers, glue, tape, markers, and scrapbooking materials. Many students can make fabulous projects with these

## Table 11
## How Parents Can Assist Students Participating in the CATCH Approach to History Fairs

1. Ask your child to explain the elements of the CATCH approach to you. This will help your child internalize these components and help you understand your child's goals and the context of the CATCH assignments.

2. Help your child stay on task by occasionally asking to see the journal, schedule, and checklist that students use as organizational tools for CATCH.

3. Read the rubrics and guidelines for quality work your child uses for the projects.

4. Assist students with transportation to libraries, museums, and other places that provide information for students in their research efforts.

5. Provide a space in your home for students to work. If your child is part of a group project, perhaps you and the other parents of students in the group could rotate using your homes to facilitate groups being able to work together after school.

6. Help supply materials needed for the visual project. If students work in a group, each set of parents could supply one or two of the elements needed. For example, in constructing an exhibit, one student's parents could provide the exhibit board, another could secure the background material and border trim, and another could supply the paper and markers needed for displaying images and signs.

7. Transport your child's visual project to the location of the history fair.

8. Assist your child in finding sources for research or resources for the visual project. For example, you might know someone who is an expert about the Spanish conquest of South America, or you might have a relative who kept letters from a loved one who served in Vietnam. Someone else you know might be willing to loan a butter churn or an arrowhead collection for a visual project.

9. Emphasize that the presentation of oneself is as important as the presentation of one's product. Dressing and behaving appropriately at the history fair demonstrates students' respect for their visitors and for the people who work hard to make the fair possible for them.

10. Listen to ideas and give constructive feedback. The work must be the students', but they can benefit from parents helping them polish their work by letting students know if their writing or visual clearly communicates their ideas.

11. Share your child's enthusiasm for producing work like a historian.

Dear Parents,

We are embarking on a great history adventure called CATCH: Capture a Time, Capture History. In this exciting activity, students will be capturing the past and presenting it in the manner of a historian. Once students have formulated a topic for this project, they will write a historical paper and represent the concepts of their papers in a visual project. The culmination of this effort will be the Colson ISD History Fair on May 12 at the Community Coliseum. At that time your child's visual project will be on display.

Although all students will research a topic and write a historical paper, their choice of visual projects will vary. One of the categories of these projects includes performances, where students will participate in a demonstration, play, monologue, speech, storytelling, reenactment, or simulated historical trial. Another category comprises exhibits, scrapbooks, and posters, while another category includes models and dioramas. Some students might choose the multimedia category and create a video, DVD, computer presentation, or Web site. Some of the students will work in groups, and some will work as individuals.

We invite you to embark on this adventure with us. Although students must work on their own, they will benefit from assistance from both home and school. Enclosed with this letter, you will find a list titled "How Parents Can Assist Students Participating in the CATCH Approach to History Fairs." We feel that your involvement with this project can be as meaningful for you as for the students.

Teachers also need your assistance if you are able to provide it. We need help with planning, organizing, arranging, and conducting the history fair. Enclosed is a list titled "How Parents Can Assist With Arranging and Conducting History Fairs." If you feel that you can help in any of these areas, please complete the enclosed form and return it to me with your child.

We will definitely appreciate any assistance you are able to give. Your contribution will make it possible to conduct a successful and effective history fair for your child, the school, and the community. Participating in CATCH can be a positive and valuable learning experience for your child. Hopefully, it will be a pleasurable and constructive occasion for you, as well.

If you have questions, please e-mail me at jharrelson@yourschooldistrict. net. We look forward to working with you.

Sincerely,

Juanita Harrelson

**Figure 56.** Sample letter to parents.

# Volunteer Services for Our History Fair

Please complete this form and return it to Juanita Harrelson via your child by January 30. We will be in touch with you as soon as we process our responses. Thank you for your help. We deeply appreciate your assistance.

Name: _____    Phone number: _____

Best time to call: _____    (Phone contact will be only if necessary)

Mailing address: _____

E-mail address: _____

*I can assist as indicated:*

| | |
|---|---|
| ❑ Serve on a planning committee | ❑ Work in a capacity at the fair from _____ to _____ |
| ❑ Enlist judges | |
| ❑ Secure community donations | ❑ Interface with the community as needed |
| ❑ Haul equipment to the fair site | ❑ Interface with management of the facility |
| ❑ Help set-up for the fair | ❑ Provide snack food for volunteers |
| ❑ Help dismantle the fair | ❑ Arrange an awards ceremony |
| ❑ Work on publicity | ❑ Make arrangements for all food concerns |
| ❑ Pick up items such as awards | ❑ Coordinate volunteers |
| ❑ Return borrowed items | ❑ Arrange to borrow items and equipment |
| ❑ Help make or distribute lunches | ❑ Other (Please describe) _____ |

If you agree to serve on a committee, when is the best time for you meet?

Comments and suggestions:

**Figure 57.** Sample volunteer form for parents.

simple materials and a little creativity, and you can ensure that none of your students are left out of the event. You might want to recruit some parents to come in and act as assistants (i.e., hot gluing models or diorama pieces, spray painting items, using any necessary power tools to build exhibits or sets) in the construction of projects, especially in grades 4 and 5.

Parents are valuable resources for assisting with history fairs and festivals. Whatever the scale of your event, parents will be able to help with planning, arranging, and conducting your history fair. Suggested parental contributions to history fairs include those listed in Table 12.

CATCH is indeed an adventure in learning for students and an agent of connection between the school, parents, and the community. All of the people involved will look back on their history fair as a time of academic growth with pride of achievement. It will be a time remembered as the day everyone regarded your students as what you have helped them become: true historians.

## Table 12
## How Parents Can Assist With Arranging and Conducting History Fairs

1. Serve on a planning committee for the history fair.

2. If a contest is involved, help secure judges.

3. Secure a place for the history event and make arrangements with the person in charge of the facility.

4. Enlist volunteers and/or be a volunteer to perform tasks in connection with the history fair. These tasks might include working at a registration table, helping participants set up their displays, manning a station of student performances or displays, making signs that show people where and when various categories of entries are on display, publicizing the history event, arranging for equipment use such as computers and microphones, and making coffee and/or providing light refreshments available for volunteers.

5. Write and print a schedule for distribution to participants and visitors to the history event.

6. Make sack lunches for the students who are participating or donate soft drinks or juice for them to have with their lunches. Collect lunches if students bring their own, write their names on them, store them in a safe place, and then distribute them at lunchtime.

7. Arrange for an awards ceremony if one is appropriate.

8. Arrange for awards. If students participate in a contest, they will receive ribbons, trophies, or some other prize such as gift certificates, or even cash if funds are available. You might volunteer to secure the awards and deliver them to the site of the awards ceremony.

9. Recruit organizations in your community to present awards to students who create projects in a category pertaining to a certain group's mission. For example, the local chapter of the Daughters of the American Revolution might want to award the best paper or project about the American Revolution or the local historical society might want to award the best paper or project about the county's history. In these cases, the organizations would make their own judgments of the projects and a representative from their agency would present the awards at a ceremony. This is an important function because it ties the community and school together and gives students an opportunity for recognition other than winning or placing in an overall contest. For example, a group of students might choose to make their visual project a demonstration of legal and illegal search and seizure as outlined in the Fourth Amendment to the Constitution. They might not place in the performance category of the history event, but they might receive an award from the local police department or bar association.

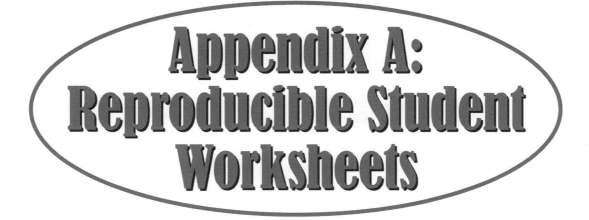

Worksheet 1: Check Your Understanding About Components of Historical Presentations. This tool is useful to help students determine if they grasp the main ideas of the concepts of historical framework and historical significance.

Worksheet 2: Joan of Arc. Use this activity to check students' ability to apply their understanding of the elements of historical framework and the meaning of historical significance.

Worksheet 3: Characteristics of a Premise. Have students read the examples and nonexamples of premises. After reading the material, have students identify three characteristics of a premise. An annotated list of characteristics follows the activity.

Worksheet 4: Is It a Premise? Once students have completed the activity in Worksheet 3, and you have discussed the concept of premises in class, give them this quiz to check for their understanding about formulating premises.

Worksheet 5: Integrating Key Components Into the Body of a Historical Paper. Give students this graphic organizer as means of outlining the body of their historical papers through weaving key components into each supporting point.

Worksheet 6: Example of Integrating Key Components Into the Body of a Historical Paper. Give this handout to students as an example of how to complete the blank graphic organizer in Worksheet 5. Point out that this example only covers one of the supporting points that might be used in a paper about Bob Hope. Remind them that if they use this tool, they will need as many copies of it as they have supporting points. Also, it is important for students to notice that some of the key components are missing from some of the points. This indicates that the key components should be relevant to the points. Sufficient coverage of the components in the historical paper as a whole is preferable to contriving a component just to make it fit a supporting point.

*Worksheet 7: Observations on "A Ghostly Gift."* Give the play, "A Ghostly Gift," (found in Appendix C) to students to read as an example of connecting a historical paper and a visual project. Although students will not have read the accompanying historical paper, ask them to take notes using the chart on this worksheet as they read the play.

# Check Your Understanding About Components of Historical Presentations

1. List four elements that make up a historical framework.

_____

_____

2. Which of these elements would reflect how a hurricane affected people along the Gulf Coast?

_____

3. Which of these elements would reflect the customs and traditions of a certain group of people?

_____

4. Which of these elements would reflect the prevailing mood of the people in a given time and place?

_____

5. Which of these elements would reflect the relationships between groups of people participating in a given event?

_____

6. When writing about a historical event, why is it important to address the historical framework of that event?

_____

_____

7. When writing about a topic, how will you determine its level of historical significance?

_____

_____

_____

_____

# Joan of Arc

Read the following story of the exploits of Joan of Arc, and see if you can identify the elements of the account's historical framework and historical significance.

## JOAN OF ARC

When Joan of Arc was a child in 1424, her country of France was overrun and occupied by England. The English were oppressive and subjected the French to raids, starvation, and death. They would not allow Charles VII, the rightful heir to the French throne, to become king because England ruled France through a man they could easily control. The people of France were devout Catholics, and so was Joan even though she was quite young. One day she had a vision that the angel Michael appeared to her in a frightening light. But, he was kind to her, and Joan was not afraid. She must have wondered why he would speak to her because he was associated with battle, and people believed that he helped Christian armies win wars. What would Joan, a peasant girl, have to do with battles?

Joan soon found out. She began to hear the voices of St. Margaret and St. Catherine. They told her that she must defeat the English. She must save France. Naturally, Joan was skeptical, but the voices persisted. Finally, she approached a man high up in the French Army and convinced him that she was supposed to lead a force against the English and have Charles crowned King of France. The Army officer was reluctant to do this because girls were not fighters, and they certainly did not tell men what to do or lead them in battle. But, in the end, he believed Joan because he was also a devout Catholic, and he did not want to defy the saints if they were giving instructions to Joan. Dressed as a boy, and calling herself Joan the Maid because she was too young for marriage, Joan led the French Army in many victorious battles and managed to have Charles crowned King of France. In every battle, Joan followed instructions she heard from St. Margaret and St. Catherine. Her fighting strategies were considered to be brilliant by all who fought with her and against her.

The people of France loved Joan and honored her for her valor. She was thrilled with all of the success and the attention, and she wanted to continue fighting until she drove the English from France. But, she no longer heard the saints' voices, and she began to act on her own. Under these circumstances, she was defeated time and again until finally the English captured her in battle.

King Charles could have paid a ransom for her and saved her life, but he was tired of all of the fighting and made a pact of peace with the English instead of rescuing Joan. The English felt humiliated by all of the defeats Joan had given them, so they planned to kill her. They put her on trial for being a witch, claiming that the voices she heard were from the devil, not from the saints. They held a trial for Joan, but they never intended to free her. They tortured her and threatened to burn her at a public execution, so in exhaustion, Joan tried to save her life by agreeing that the voices she heard were indeed from the devil. The English relented, but said that she had to stay in prison the rest of her life.

**Statue of Joan of Arc in New Orleans**

In her cell, Joan heard the voices of St. Margaret and St. Catherine again. Joan became overwhelmed with guilt for declaring that she had heard from the devil instead of the saints. Joan knew that she could not live with this betrayal to the saints, so she told the judge that she had signed a confession in fear. She had to tell the truth. She had heard the saints talking to her.

In 1431, a guard of English soldiers tied Joan to a post in the marketplace and scattered flammable brush around her feet. They lit the fire and through the smoke and flames, Joan cried out to her saints until she died. She was 19 years old. After her death, even the English knew that killing Joan had been wrong. The French were ashamed that they had not protected her. King Charles was shocked by how unfair her trial was, and he ordered a new one. Though she was dead, she was found innocent of being a witch.

After Joan was burned at the stake, her countrymen began to rally against the English, and eventually completely drove them out of France. Today, Joan of Arc is considered to be a great heroine. There are statues of her all over France, and in 1920, Pope Benedict XV declared her to be Catholic saint. Artwork, movies, plays, and books depict her as a brave savior of her people and true follower of God.

No one knows if France would have eventually driven the English out of their land without the inspiration of Joan the Maid, but it is clearly evident that this young girl changed the hearts and lives of both her friends and enemies.

## SOURCES:

Bull, Angela. *Joan of Arc*. New York: DK Publishing, 2000.

*Joan of Arc*. Available from http://en.wikipedia.org/wiki/Joan_of_Arc. Accessed 10 May, 2007.

## HISTORICAL FRAMEWORK

What is the historical framework of the story of Joan of Arc? Fill in the chart below with your answers.

| IDEAS AND VALUES: | GEOGRAPHICAL INFLUENCE: |
|---|---|
| SOCIAL ISSUES: | CULTURAL ISSUES: |

## HISTORICAL SIGNIFICANCE

Write a 3–5 sentence paragraph explaining the historical significance of the story of Joan of Arc.

# Characteristics of a Premise

Read the following examples of premises and nonpremises. As your read the statements, list three characteristics of a premise that emerge.

**Focus:** *The Contribution of Navajo Code Talkers*

| PREMISE | NONPREMISE |
|---|---|
| At a crucial time for American Forces in the Pacific, a group of Navajos developed and implemented the most significant military code used during World War II. | During World War II, a group of Navajos developed and used a communication code based on their language. |

**Focus:** *The Atomic Bomb*

| Premise | Nonpremise |
|---|---|
| The decision to use the atomic bomb had the greatest impact of any decision the American government made during the 20th century. | The United States dropped atomic bombs on two Japanese cities during World War II. |

**Focus:** *The Hope That Bob Brought to American Armed Forces*

| Premise | Nonpremise |
|---|---|
| Bob Hope played a significant role in boosting the morale of U.S. troops stationed in combat zones during World War II through his commitment to bringing entertaining shows and by assuring his audience that they were fighting to save the American way of life and American values. | Bob Hope entertained thousands of troops fighting in the Pacific Theater with his humor and his cast of famous performers of the day. |

**What are three characteristics of a premise you found in the above statements?**

1. _____

2. _____

3. _____

# Is It a Premise?

Determine if each statement below is a premise or nonpremise by writing P (premise) or N (nonpremise) on the line next to each.

_____    1.  Barbarian tribes played a significant role in the eventual fall of the Roman Empire.

_____    2.  King Tut's tomb contained Egyptian artifacts of his era.

_____    3.  Although some people disagreed, establishing internment camps to hold Japanese, German, and Italian Americans was necessary for the safety of other Americans during World War II.

_____    4.  Requiring Native American children to attend English-speaking boarding schools was the best solution for acclimating these children to being loyal citizens of the United States.

_____    5.  The Chinese people have various customs and traditions for celebrating the New Year.

_____    6.  Many African nations have gained their independence from European nations that once claimed their lands.

_____    7.  The Mayan civilization was far superior to the civilizations established along the Mississippi River.

_____    8.  Pennsylvania was the most appealing of the original 13 American colonies because it was founded on Quaker principles.

_____    9.  England owes its defeat of the Spanish Armada to the leadership of Queen Elizabeth.

_____    10. Gerald Ford succeeded Richard Nixon as President of the United States when Nixon resigned.

Name:_____ Date:_____

# Integrating Key Components Into the Body of a Historical Paper

Title of Paper: _____

Premise Statement: _____

_____

Supporting Point: _____

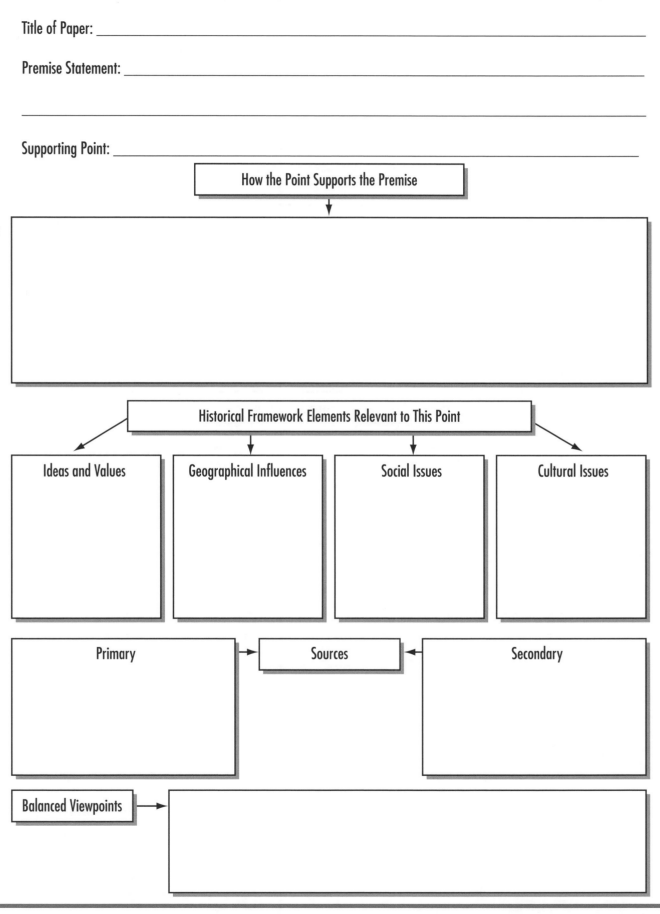

| How the Point Supports the Premise |

| Historical Framework Elements Relevant to This Point |

| Ideas and Values | Geographical Influences | Social Issues | Cultural Issues |

| Primary | Sources | Secondary |

| Balanced Viewpoints |

# Example of Integrating Key Components Into the Body of a Historical Paper

**Title of Paper:** The Hope That Bob Brought

**Premise Statement:** Bob Hope played a significant role in boosting the morale of U.S. troops stationed in combat zones during World War II through his commitment to bringing entertaining shows and by assuring his audience that they were fighting to save the American way of life and values.

**Supporting Point:** 1. Bob Hope was deeply committed to the enterprise.

How the Point Supports the Premise

Doing a show for troops based in California made Bob Hope realize the deep level of sacrifice the troops were making on behalf of the American people. He knew that if they could make this sacrifice, so could he.

During the war, Bob Hope broadcast 135 of his variety shows from military bases rather than from the comfort and convenience of a radio studio in the states. This illustrates his depth of his commitment to boosting the morale of military personnel.

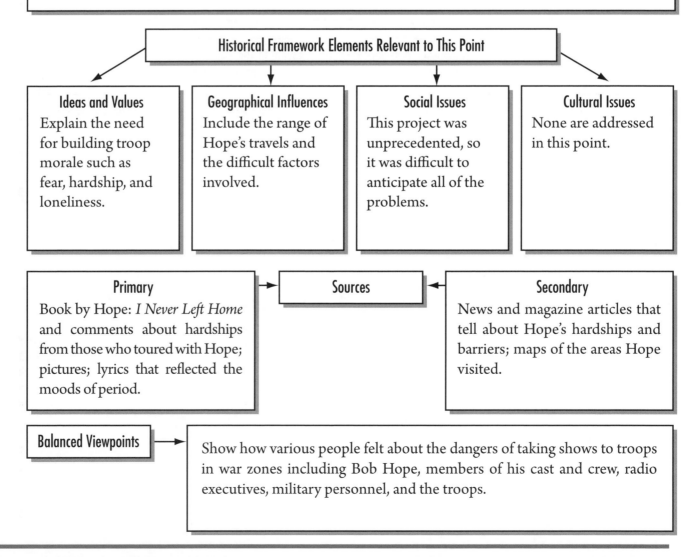

**Historical Framework Elements Relevant to This Point**

| Ideas and Values | Geographical Influences | Social Issues | Cultural Issues |
|---|---|---|---|
| Explain the need for building troop morale such as fear, hardship, and loneliness. | Include the range of Hope's travels and the difficult factors involved. | This project was unprecedented, so it was difficult to anticipate all of the problems. | None are addressed in this point. |

**Sources**

| Primary | Secondary |
|---|---|
| Book by Hope: *I Never Left Home* and comments about hardships from those who toured with Hope; pictures; lyrics that reflected the moods of period. | News and magazine articles that tell about Hope's hardships and barriers; maps of the areas Hope visited. |

**Balanced Viewpoints** → Show how various people felt about the dangers of taking shows to troops in war zones including Bob Hope, members of his cast and crew, radio executives, military personnel, and the troops.

# Observations on "A Ghostly Gift"

**CATCH Topic:** Societal Reactions to Technological Changes

**Historical Paper's Title:** The Demise of Port Almuda

**Background:** Although the people and place of this play are fictitious, it illustrates how the premise, historical significance, and historical framework of a historical paper can weave together in a visual project. The overall theme of change and people's adaptation or lack of adaptation to change has been prevalent throughout history, and many settlements have become ghost towns as a result of the circumstances and attitudes of the characters presented in the play.

**Instructions:** As you read the play, fill in the spaces below with your observations of the components of historical paper.

| PROBABLE PREMISE |
| --- |
| |
| **HISTORICAL SIGNIFICANCE** |
| |
| **HISTORICAL FRAMEWORK:**<br>*Ideas and values* |
| *Geographical influences* |
| *Social issues* |
| *Cultural issues* |

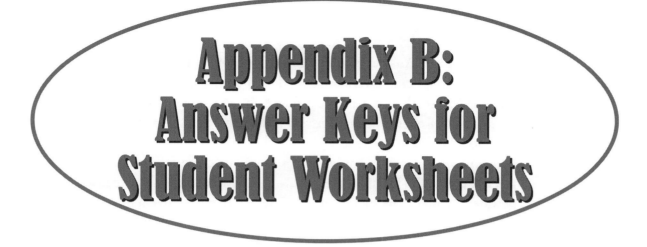

# Appendix B: Answer Keys for Student Worksheets

## Worksheet 1—Check Your Understanding About Components of Historical Presentations

1. Ideas and values of people involved in an event; geographical influences; social issues; cultural issues (can be listed in any order)

2. Geographical influences

3. Cultural issues

4. Ideas and values of people involved in an event

5. Social issues

6. Any answer that expresses the following idea is acceptable: It is important to capture the way people thought in a given place and time period, because it is necessary to understand their circumstances and why and how they acted as they did. It also is necessary to understand how and why they were different from us so that we will not impose our ideas and ways of life on them.

7. Any answer that expresses the following idea is acceptable: The historical significance of an event indicates how that event has made an impact over time. For example, an idea that was once considered unusual is now acceptable, or the issues related to the event continue to remain issues over time, or the event continues to have an influence on our lives today.

# Worksheet 2—Joan of Arc

## HISTORICAL FRAMEWORK

- *Ideas and values*: Answer may be similar to the following: During Joan's childhood, the French were oppressed by the English, but they feared the English, so they did not feel that they were able to drive their enemy away. Religious beliefs greatly influenced the way people lived and thought.
- *Geographical influences*: Answer may be similar to the following: The place was France. The time was 1424–1431. Although a vast expanse of water separated the two countries, England managed to occupy and control France. The terrain of battlegrounds required Joan to use brilliant fighting strategies.
- *Social issues*: Answer may be similar to the following: Most people were poor because of English oppression. Many problems, such as starvation, that come with poverty were prevalent. Females were not normally considered to be leaders or have significant influence.
- *Cultural issues*: Answer may be similar to the following: People believed that witches were active among them. Torture was an acceptable form of punishment.

## HISTORICAL SIGNIFICANCE

Answer may be similar to the following: Joan of Arc was a significant figure in history because she inspired her people to take a stand against their oppressors and drive the English out of France, making that country independent of English domination. The significance of her deeds is shown by the attention she has received through the centuries since her death.

# Worksheet 3—Characteristics of a Premise

Students should have found the following characteristics of a premise statement. Teachers should discuss the explanations of each characteristic below with students to help them use these characteristics to develop their own premise statements.

1. *Premises make an assertion that needs supporting evidence and interpretation.* Words like "most significant" and "greatest impact" require an explanation

of why and how one course of action was preferable to another. What difference did the Navajo code make to battle outcomes? How was deciding to use the atomic bomb of such great significance? How could making people laugh in the course of daily life and death struggles help the war effort?

2. *Each premise calls for a conclusion that emerges from evidence.* A premise identifies a declaration that someone may or may not accept. As historians, students will present evidence that leads to a conclusion that their premises are reasonable.

3. *Each premise statement offers an organizational tool for writing a historical paper.* For example, Bob Hope lived a full and eventful life. He made many movies and won many awards for his work. But, a paper that follows the worksheet's premise statement about Bob Hope will limit its content to how Bob Hope's boosting troop morale made an impact on Americans fighting in World War II. Limiting the scope of the entertainer's contributions will assist students in developing the scope of their papers.

## Worksheet 4—Is It a Premise?

1. P
2. N
3. P
4. P
5. N
6. N
7. P
8. P
9. P
10. N

The premise statements make assertions that require supporting evidence and call for a conclusion. The nonpremise statements are facts that require no supporting evidence.

## Worksheet 5—Integrating Key Components Into the Body of a Historical Paper

Answers will vary.

# Worksheet 7—Observations of "A Ghostly Gift"

## PROBABLE PREMISE

Callie said, "It's not just new ideas or new products that make an impact, it's what people do with new products and new ideas that make a difference to a town or even to an individual." This could serve well as the premise statement.

## HISTORICAL SIGNIFICANCE

Throughout history, people have influenced the lives of each other with emphatic results. Knowing when and how to react to change brought about by advancing technology has been a problem among people in communities and societies since the beginning of mankind. The contrast between Ezra Franklin and Ernest Malone illustrates this concept.

## HISTORICAL FRAMEWORK

- *Ideas and values*: People in Port Almuda were aware of the transportation changes taking place, but not everyone regarded these changes as advantages. Some of the citizens were reluctant to adjust because of personal and business reasons. During this time, as in every age, each technological advance brought new problems such as the loss of nutritional value in machine-ground corn. People were forced to decide whether to go with what appeared to be progress or continue in their old way of doing things.

- *Geographical influences*: In the past, being located on a broad and deep river was an advantage to the people of Port Almuda. But, those waters were changing just as technology was changing. Some of the widest rivers were reduced to trickles because of the need for dams and reservoirs in other locations.

- *Social issues*: The town's economy was dependent on timber and commerce. When a decision had to be made about future transportation of goods and lumber, people divided according to their own self-interests.

- *Cultural issues*: The wealthier people of the town felt that they had the right to determine the town's direction. They did not want to consider how their decisions would affect people they thought were beneath their social station. This attitude affected the outcome of the town's future.

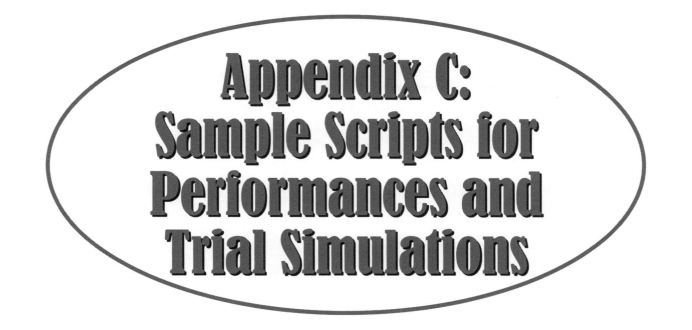
# Appendix C:
# Sample Scripts for
# Performances and
# Trial Simulations

# The Pelfreys Pitch In
## By Helen Bass

**Adapted with permission by the Texas Education Agency.**
**Copyright © Texas Education Agency. All Rights Reserved.**

## ARTIFACTS

Washboard and small tub
Ration book
Telegram
Phonograph record
*Life* Magazine from World War II era with advertisements

## SET

There are no actual doors, windows, or walls.

## PROPS

Artifacts
Table
Three chairs

## CAST

Martha Pelfrey (teenage daughter)
Joey Pelfrey (preteen son)
Rosie Pelfrey (Mother of Martha and Joey)
Western Union messenger

(The scene opens with Martha washing a blouse on a washboard in a small metal tub sitting on a table. A song popular in World War II times is playing loudly in the background. Martha is scrubbing and lip syncing dramatically. Some possible song titles include: "I'll Be Seeing You"; "Ac-cent-tchu-ate the Positive"; "Boogie Woogie Bugle Boy"; "Don't Get Around Much Anymore"; "I Don't Want to Set the World on Fire"; "I'll Walk Alone"; "Is You Is or Is You Ain't My Baby"; "It's Been a Long, Long Time"; "Long Ago (and Far Away)"; "Praise the Lord and Pass the Ammunition"; "There's a Star Spangled Banner Waving Somewhere"; "Why Do They Call a Private a Private?"; and "You'd Be So Nice to Come Home to")

| | |
|---|---|
| *Joey:* | (Bursting in the room yelling at his sister) Hey, Sis! What's all the racket? I can hear that dumb song all the way down to the corner. I bet they can hear it over the bombs in Germany. Shut it up, ok?! |
| *Martha:* | Don't tell me what to do, Joey Pelfrey, or I just might tell Mama that you didn't pick up the string and stuff this week. Old Mrs. Mayfield mentioned to me today how wild you are without a father around to keep you in line. |
| *Joey:* | (Racing out of the room and immediately returning with a record) Turn it down, or I'm going to break this record right in half. |
| *Martha:* | (Throwing down her washing and chasing her brother) Don't you dare break that record! It's my favorite and I'll never be able to replace it. |
| *Joey:* | Ha! You don't even know what it is. You can't see the label. |
| *Martha:* | I can see the stars coming out of your head after I bop you with a frying pan. |
| *Joey:* | (Chanting) I'm gonna break it, I'm gonna break it…. |
| *Martha:* | If you even scratch it, I'll charge you 50 cents for it. Scratching is the same as breaking 'cause it won't play all the way through. |
| *Joey:* | Fifty cents! The dumb thing only cost 35 cents. |
| *Martha:* | I'll charge you for insult! (Stopping to catch her breath) Look, Joey. I'll turn down the record player 'cause Mama will be home in a minute, but don't think you've won any kind of battle. |
| *Joey:* | Sure, Marty. |
| *Martha:* | Don't call me that. I'm Martha. Remember that! (Exits) |

(The music stops)

| | |
|---|---|
| *Joey:* | Hey, look! The new issue of *Life* Magazine came today! (Picks it up from the table) Wonder if any new cars have come out. |
| *Martha:* | (Entering) Say, Joey, have you heard that there's a war on? If you had picked up the string for that victory project you have going at school, you would know that. They are cutting back on car production, not making new ones. |
| *Joey:* | I know that! All the metal has to go for planes and tanks. |
| *Martha:* | (Wistfully) Yeah, and ships like the ones Mama helps make at the Navy yard and the ship that Daddy is stationed on. |

**Joey:** (Quietly) Yeah. Hey, would you look at this: Chevrolet's ad. It's not about cars at all. Doesn't even show a car. It's about a conservation plan—conserve tires, conserve gas, conserve oil, on and on. Everything's about the war. I'm sick of it.

**Martha:** I know, Joey. So am I. Look at this old washboard. It says, "Victory Glass. Use this washboard made of materials not needed for defense and help win the war." And, oh my goodness, look at that ad. Even Kleenex tells you how you can be patriotic.

**Joey:** Yeah, listen to this, "When sending the boys homemade cookies, fill crevices of the box with Kleenex. Prevents jiggling and breaking!" Gee whiz . . .

**Martha:** Look out the window, Joey. Here comes Mama. Oh, I have to get the washing off the table so we can have dinner. (Quickly removes the washtub and washboard)

**Joey:** You might forget about that. She's not carrying any groceries.

**Martha:** But, she took all of our ration books with her today. She must have had enough stamps for something. She looks awfully tired. Maybe she just couldn't drag herself to the store.

**Joey:** She always looks tired. That's because she does a man's job with the war on. I call her Rosie the Riveter, behind her back of course.

**Rosie:** (Entering and smiling with forced cheeriness) Well, hello, my little angels. How's everything going?

**Martha:** What's wrong, Mama?

**Rosie:** Now, Martha. What makes you think something's wrong?

**Joey:** No groceries. Fake smile.

**Rosie:** My, my . . . this war has made cynics even of my children. Always expecting the worse. I thought that I was being a good example of optimism, but . . .

**Martha:** Quit stalling. Tell us, Mama.

(Everyone sits in the chairs)

**Rosie:** It's just a rumor mind you.

**Joey:** Go on, Mama.

**Rosie:** Well, down at the shipyard today, we got the news that about five of our ships in one of the fleets were blown out of the Pacific Ocean by Japanese fighter planes.

| Martha: | Is it the part of the Pacific that Daddy's in? |
|---|---|
| Rosie: | I don't know. Actually, your father hasn't been allowed to let us know his exact location for a long time now. |
| Joey: | Maybe he's not in the Pacific at all. Maybe his crew is on shore right now. |
| Rosie: | Hopefully you're right, Joey. The Pacific is a mighty big ocean, and there are hundreds of ships out there, and perhaps it's all just talk after all. |
| Martha: | When was this supposed to have happened? |
| Rosie: | A few days ago, I think. |
| Martha: | Whew . . . that's good, right? If anything had happened to Daddy, we would surely have heard by now. |

(There is a knock at the door)

| Rosie: | (Calling out) Who is it? |
|---|---|
| Messenger: | Western Union, ma'am. |
| Martha: | (Whispering anxiously) A telegram! Not a telegram! Mama, don't answer it. |
| Rosie: | We have to know, Martha. (Rises and opens the door) |
| Messenger: | Good evening, ma'am. |
| Rosie: | Good evening. Do you have something for me? |
| Messenger: | If you're Mrs. Pelfrey, then it's for you, ma'am. It's a telegram. Will you please sign here? |

(Rosie signs)

| Messenger: | Hope it's not bad news. Well, good night. |
|---|---|
| Rosie: | Oh, just a minute. Martha, will you get a dime out of my purse and tip this messenger? |
| Martha: | Yes, ma'am. (Gets the money and gives it to the messenger.) |
| Messenger: | Sure thank you now. (Exits) |

(Rosie and Martha sit. All three stare at the telegram)

| Joey: | Guess you better open it, Mama. |
|---|---|

| Rosie: | (Opens the telegram and reads) Dear Rosie, Martha, and Joey. Stop. Was slightly injured. Stop. Am in hospital in Hawaii. Stop. Will be home soon. Stop. Do not worry. Stop. |
|---|---|
| Joey: | Daddy's coming home! |
| Rosie: | He's injured. Wonder what that means? |
| Martha: | Slightly, Mama! Slightly injured. Daddy's coming home! |
| Rosie: | He sent it himself. No one wrote it for him. That's a good sign, isn't it? |
| Joey: | It sure is, Mama! It sure is. |
| Rosie: | Goodness me. I'm about to let you children starve to death. First, I couldn't go to the grocery store because I was so worried. And now, I'm so relieved, I'm about to forget about dinner. Joey, get the ration books out of my purse. Get one that still has some meat stamps. And, get my coin purse. |
| Joey: | Hot dog! Maybe hot dogs? |
| Rosie: | No, run down to the corner store and get a can of MOR. |
| Martha: | MOR, that canned chopped-up-and-spit-out-again ham? Gee whiz, Mama, can't we do better than that? |
| Rosie: | They say our servicemen eat it, and we have no business eating better than they do. Now hurry, Joey. Martha, get a jar of our Victory Garden green beans out of the cupboard. I'll get the pots and pans ready. |
| Martha: | And Joey, it's important to come back right away. We have to clean up the kitchen before the blackout tonight. |
| Rosie: | Are we having air raid practice tonight? Oh yes, I remember now. |
| Joey: | What time? |
| Martha: | 8:00 Pacific War Time. All lights out by then! |
| Joey: | And, no loud record players. Ha! Ha! |
| Martha: | Get out of here, Joey. |
| Rosie: | Children . . . |

# A Ghostly Gift
## By Helen Bass

## CHARACTERS

**People of the Present:**
Callie Malone: Recent high school graduate
Jacob Malone: Grandfather of Callie

**People of the Past:**
Ezra Franklin: merchant in Port Almuda
Jewel Franklin: wife of Ezra
Ernest Malone: reporter for the *Port Almuda Banner*, a weekly newspaper

## SETTING

The play takes place at the Grand Almuda, a hotel alternating between being a ruin in the current day ghost town of Port Almuda and a prosperous establishment in the thriving town of Port Almuda in 1874.

(Callie and Jacob enter from stage left and stand in front of a dilapidated structure with a sign hanging askew and reading "Grand Almuda." A large opening covered by a sheet of tarpaulin takes up most of the set. The tarp is attached to cords that allow it to rise up as a window shade. As they take their places in front of the hotel, Jacob is standing left of the tarp, and Callie is standing to the right of the tarp)

| | |
|---|---|
| *Callie:* | Granddad, I just don't understand how a trip to this dusty old town is a high school graduation present. Don't get me wrong. I know I can trust ol' Jacob Malone to come up with some pretty amazing surprises. You're certainly known for your innovative gifts, and I'm grateful for anything you give me, but what's there to see or do here? |
| *Jacob:* | Well, young Callie Malone, this is a ghost town, so nobody really does much of anything here anymore, but it was once a pretty prosperous town. See the river over there? |
| *Callie:* | Yes. |
| *Jacob:* | Port Almuda was once a major port in these parts. Merchandise was brought in from all over the United States, and timber from the surrounding area was shipped out. |

| Callie: | You mean people actually used that river for shipping? What kind of boat could get down that little stream? |
|---|---|
| Jacob: | That little stream is the Optimist River, once much wider and deeper before they built the damn over near Forest City. Steamboats used to bring goods and passengers in and out of here daily from about 1840 to 1890. |
| Callie: | I guess that's kind of interesting, Granddad, but what does this ghost town have to do with me? |
| Jacob: | Well, Callie, you're getting ready to go to college and major in business, aren't you? |
| Callie: | That's right. I'd like to get into marketing. It's a pretty exciting field with so many new products being invented all the time. Somebody needs to sell the public on those things, and I want to be one of those people. |
| Jacob: | Have you ever thought about how those things got to be new to people and how someday all that new stuff could become old and useless? Then, what will you do? |
| Callie: | There will always be new things to take their place. Computers replaced typewriters. Color television replaced black and white TVs. Cell phones are taking over other phone systems. I know about change. I think it's exciting. I'm always ready for change. That's an advantage of youth. |
| Jacob: | True, but how will you know when to change and what to change? Is all change good? What happens if you don't recognize when to take in something new? What if you take in something new before people are ready for it, and you go bust? How do you know you aren't replacing quality with quantity? Remember when you and your family visited that old mill on your vacation trip last summer? |
| Callie: | Oh, yes. Hanley's Mill. It was a beautiful place, and it used to grind corn for the local farmers. But, it could only grind about 12 bushels a day, and when the mechanical mills came in, they could grind thousands of bushels a day, so the mill became defunct. |
| Jacob: | Right, and what did the docent at the mill tell you was the trouble with that arrangement? |
| Callie: | He said that the rollers in the mechanical mills got so hot they took a large portion of nutrition out of the corn, but they use them anyway because they can produce so much more corn than water-powered |

mills and therefore sell more corn to a much larger market. Are we getting around to the purpose of visiting this ghost town?

*Jacob:* Maybe changing one thing drastically changes other things, so people have to make decisions about what they want the most. In the case of the mills, people decided that quantity was more important than retaining nutrients. Maybe something like that happened in Port Almuda. Maybe some of the people didn't recognize when to make a major change.

*Callie:* So, what you're saying is that I'm right about being ready for change.

*Jacob:* Maybe.

*Callie:* You have more to tell me, don't you? I bet it has something to do with this dead old town.

*Jacob:* Maybe.

*Callie:* It has something to do with people and change, I guess.

*Jacob:* Maybe.

*Callie:* I know you want me to learn something from this trip, but I don't think you're going to tell me outright. I'm going to make a guess based on what you've said so far and see where that leads me. Okay, here's my guess: It's not just new ideas or new products that make an impact, it's what people do with new products and new ideas that make a difference to a town or even to an individual. Am I on the right track?

*Jacob:* Maybe.

(Strains of violin music, soft laughter and subdued clinking of glass and china edge into the conversation)

*Callie:* What's that?

*Jacob:* Why don't you raise that tarp over the window and see?

(Callie carefully raises the tarp in front of the hotel set to reveal a party scene in the Grand Almuda. In the foreground Ezra and Jewel Franklin are dressed in elegant late 19th century clothing. They are holding china plates bearing small cakes. In the near background, Ernest Malone is standing with his back to the Franklins as though in conversation with an unseen person. He is dressed in modest 19th-century clothing)

| | |
|---|---|
| *Callie:* | Granddad! This is too weird! What's going on? |
| *Jacob:* | Shh! Listen to the conversation. |
| *Jewel:* | Oh, Ezra! I just love these New Year's parties at the Grand Almuda. The Dittlingers really know how to entertain. It's a great way to bring in the year 1874. I just know it's going to be wonderful year! |
| *Ezra:* | Alfred Dittlinger might be the richest man in Port Almuda with his booming timber business and all, but I'm the most influential. Just look at all these fine clothes the people are wearing. They bought them all from me. And, the hotel bought this china we're holding from me. Yes, sir! It's my contacts with those big firms in New York that keeps this town in the best goods available. |
| *Jewel:* | Well, there's no question about that, dear. Franklin's Mercantile sells the best of everything. It's far and away the most wonderful store on the Optimist River. Oh, look, there's Juanita in that yellow taffeta gown you ordered for her. She looks just lovely. |
| *Ezra:* | Humph! On a banker's salary, her husband could have bought pure silk. |
| *Jewel:* | Do we have any more silk in any of our warehouses? I fancy having a red silk shawl with miles and miles of black silk fringe dangling from its edges. |
| *Ezra:* | Might have some. Uh, oh. Look out, Jewel. Young Ernest Malone is coming our way. |
| *Jewel:* | Oh dear, why does he have to bother us? I hope he doesn't quote us in his filthy old weekly newspaper. You know how his story about those boys breaking into the dormitory of the female college upset everyone. I don't trust him at all. |

(Ernest approaches the Franklins and begins a conversation)

| | |
|---|---|
| *Ernest:* | Good evening, Mr. and Mrs. Franklin. Fine party, isn't it? |
| *Ezra:* | Yes, it is Mr. Malone. I didn't realize you knew the Dittlinger family. |
| *Ernest:* | I suppose you mean that I'm not really worthy of hobnobbing with Port Almuda's upper crust of society? |
| *Jewel:* | Oh, Mr. Malone. Don't be so sensitive. Are you here as a reporter for the Port Almuda Banner, or are you a guest? |
| *Ernest:* | Well, I'm not in charge of the society page. Ellen Ragsdale takes care of that each week. You know her, I'm sure. |

| Jewel: | Of course. Everyone knows Mrs. Ragsdale. After all, her husband is president of the boy's academy and our mayor. |
|---|---|
| Ernest: | Speaking of the mayor, that reminds me of the railroad issue. Mr. Franklin, are you still set against having the railroad come through Port Almuda? |
| Ezra: | I certainly am. |
| Ernest: | But, wouldn't a railroad running through town bring you more business? Your merchandise could arrive faster than by steamboat. The population of the town probably would eventually increase, and you surely would have more customers. |
| Ezra: | The system we have in place works just fine. My warehouses are down by the docks, and my boys can easily unload the goods from the steamboats and load up the warehouses. I know all the people involved in the shipping business and have all my contacts established. Business is booming. Why upset something that works so perfectly when you don't know how working with railroad people will turn out? |
| Jewel: | Besides, railroads bring in all kinds of riffraff, a really low-class people. I got a letter from my sister over in Ball County recently, and she said the trains belch sooty smoke and make so much noise it fairly disrupts the tranquility of a peaceful town. And, the people they deposit onto the depot platforms are sometimes tramps. Why if one of those people appeared in our store, I think I'd faint. |
| Ernest: | Port Almuda has poor people in town right now. What do you do when they come into your store? |
| Jewel: | Well, since I don't work in the store, I don't know. But, I'm sure that if there are people like that in this town, they know that they can't afford to buy anything in Franklin's Mercantile, so they just don't come in. Strangers might not know that. |
| Ernest: | Mr. Franklin, Mr. Dittlinger is working hard to get the railroad to come through town. He thinks it will be good for his timber business. Seems like the two of you would have business interests in common. |
| Ezra: | Well, our businesses are of a different nature. See, he only sells one thing: timber. His market is mostly out of town. And, he doesn't transport much of anything into town. He buys everything he needs from me. My market is in this town. I've helped make Port Almuda a major commercial center for this part of the state. His business gives people of the town a few jobs, but they are mostly laborers |

| | |
|---|---|
| | and don't have any influence. People won't see things his way. The real decision makers of this town depend on me for everything they own. They'll see things my way. Wait and see. |
| Ernest: | You might be right, Mr. Franklin. However, many people predict that steamboat transportation will be a thing of the past in just a few years. Railroads are speedier and even more reliable. Besides, not every area has rivers nearby that can support steamboats. Railroads can cross any kind of terrain and connect the whole nation. It will be interesting to see how things are going in this town 20 years from now. |
| Jewel: | Well, I can tell you that 100 years from now our descendants will thank us for preserving the cultural climate of Port Almuda because my husband and other reasonable people will defeat any attempts to run a filthy railroad through our genteel and prestigious town. |
| Ernest: | May I quote you on that, Mrs. Franklin? |

(Ernest and the Franklins freeze in place)

| | |
|---|---|
| Jacob: | Callie, you can lower the tarp now. I think that's all we'll get to see of Port Almuda in its heyday. |

(Callie lowers the tarp)

| | |
|---|---|
| Callie: | (In awe) Granddad, how did you do that? |
| Jacob: | Do what? |
| Callie: | Do what? How did you produce people who lived more than 100 years ago? That's what! |
| Jacob: | Well, Callie, my dear, I can't tell you. I wouldn't want to spoil my reputation for surprises. |
| Callie: | Granddad! Tell me! |
| Jacob: | (Chuckling) No, Callie, you tell me. What do you think about your guess now? |
| Callie: | My guess? Oh, in all the eeriness I almost forgot. Well, actually, I think the Franklins confirmed my idea. They showed that new products and new ideas don't make an impact all by themselves. It's what people do with new products and new ideas that make a difference. Well, I think that's what happened in Port Almuda. We know today that railroads did replace steamboat transportation, and |

|        |                                                                                                                                                                                                                                                       |
|--------|-------------------------------------------------------------------------------------------------------------------------------------------------------------------------------------------------------------------------------------------------------|
|        | we know that the railroad didn't come through this town. At least, I don't see any tracks.                                                                                                                                                             |
| *Jacob:* | You're right. The town voted to turn down a railroad company's proposal to come through Port Almuda, and they missed their opportunity. Steamboats became a way of the past as river transportation became inadequate compared to railroads. And, young Ernest Malone was right. |
| *Callie:* | Ernest Malone. Hmm, Granddad, is he our ancestor?                                                                                                                                                                                                     |
| *Jacob:* | He sure is. He's your great-great-great-grandfather.                                                                                                                                                                                                  |
| *Callie:* | How do you know about him?                                                                                                                                                                                                                            |
| *Jacob:* | Well, my dear, that's another story and another surprise.                                                                                                                                                                                             |
| *Callie:* | Granddad?                                                                                                                                                                                                                                             |
| *Jacob:* | Yes, Callie?                                                                                                                                                                                                                                          |
| *Callie:* | Thank you for my graduation present. (She hugs Jacob)                                                                                                                                                                                                 |
| *Jacob:* | You're very welcome. I enjoyed the trip too. Time to get back to a live town?                                                                                                                                                                         |
| *Callie:* | You bet. Let's go, but I'll never forget this ghostly gift.                                                                                                                                                                                           |

( Jacob and Callie exit arm in arm and pantomime talking as they go)

# The Trial of John C. Calhoun
## By Helen Bass

(*Note:* This trial is scripted as an example of conducting a virtual historical trial. Your students' trial will be spontaneous and conducted from their historical paper preparation.)

## TRIAL PARTICIPANTS

Judge Thomas Scott Williams, Chief Justice of the Supreme Court of Connecticut
Unnamed clerk
Announcer (can be student unrelated to trial or teacher)
Prosecuting Attorneys: Henry Clay and Daniel Webster
Prosecution Witnesses: President Andrew Jackson and Joel Roberts Poinsett
Defendant: John C. Calhoun
Defense Attorneys: Robert Hayne and George McDuffie
Defense Witnesses: John C. Calhoun and James Hamilton

## PROPS

*For the judge:* copy of the Constitutional definition of treason, list of stipulated facts of the case
*For the clerk:* Bible for swearing in witnesses
*For evidence:* copy of an excerpt from the "South Carolina Exposition and Protest," medallion, copy of an excerpt from the "South Carolina Ordinance of Nullification"

*Announcer:* Welcome to our virtual historical trial. This trial is called virtual because it never actually took place, but the circumstances surrounding the trial did occur. President Andrew Jackson did publicly accuse former Vice President John C. Calhoun of treason because of Calhoun's role in the Nullification Crisis. Calhoun's home state of South Carolina passed an ordinance to nullify, or disregard, the tariff laws they felt were destroying the economy of the Southern states. To back up this decree, the state voted to build up its army to fight the federal government if necessary. Was John C. Calhoun responsible for this state of affairs? Was he actually guilty of treason? Perhaps this trial will settle that matter after all this time. The year of the trial is 1835. The nullification crisis ended 2 years earlier, but in this scenario President Jackson does not want to leave office without attempting to convict his former vice president of treason.

**Clerk:** All rise for the honorable Judge Williams.

(Everyone rises)

**Judge:** (Entering and sitting at the bench) You may be seated.

(Everyone sits)

**Judge:** People of the jury, we are gathered here to determine if John Caldwell Calhoun, former Vice President of the United States and current senator from South Carolina in the United States Congress, is guilty of treason against the United States. The guideline for your decision is no less than the Constitution of the United States. This is what that document says about treason: "Article III, Section 3. Treason against the United States, shall consist only in levying war against them, or in adhering to their enemies, giving them aid and comfort. No person shall be convicted of treason unless on the testimony of two witnesses to the same overt act, or on confession in open court." (He pauses) In this case, it is the burden of the prosecution to show that John C. Calhoun has tried to bring war against the United States. The prosecution must provide two witnesses who have personal knowledge that the defendant committed this act, or the defendant must confess to this act. Your charge is to determine if the prosecution has fulfilled these conditions beyond a reasonable doubt. (He pauses) Now, gentlemen of the prosecution and defense, I have before me a list of the stipulated facts of this case, and it is my understanding that you both agree that these are facts and that they pertain to this case.

**Clay:** The prosecution so agrees, your Honor.

**Hayne:** The defense also agrees, your Honor.

**Judge:** Very well, I will read the stipulated facts to the jury. Fact one: In 1828, when he was Vice President of the United States, John C. Calhoun secretly wrote a document titled "South Carolina Exposition and Protest." Fact two: This document encouraged South Carolina to nullify or refuse to obey the Tariff Act of 1828. Fact three: At that time the South Carolina Legislature did not vote to nullify the Tariff Act, but it did do so after the Tariff Act of 1832 was passed, and the state also voted to build up its army to enforce its stance against obeying the act. Fact four: When President Andrew Jackson discovered that John C. Calhoun was the author of the "South Carolina Exposition and Protest," he accused then Vice President Calhoun of treason but did not bring official charges against him. Fact five: Official charges are now being brought against Senator Calhoun because of the escalation of sectionalism issues in Congress. Because both parties agree to these facts, we will proceed with the trial. The prosecution may present an opening statement.

**Clay:** (Rises) Thank you, your Honor. (Stands before the jury) People of the jury, I would like to introduce my esteemed co-counsel and myself. I am Senator Henry Clay from Kentucky. I have served in the Senate for many years and have earned the nickname "The Great Compromiser" because I have a deep desire for our Congressmen to be fair to each other and to the people we represent. I work hard to avoid conflict in our Congressional matters. You have surely heard of my co-counsel, Senator Daniel Webster from Massachusetts. He has also served in the Senate for many years and has become famous in two areas. He is an accomplished attorney and has taken part in many important cases in our country. He is also a famous orator. You might have heard how he soundly defeated Senator Robert Hayne in a Congressional debate. By the way, that gentleman is seated at the defense table as one of the defendant's lawyers.

**Hayne:** (Rises) Your Honor, I object to this personal affront on the grounds that it has no relevance to this case.

**Judge:** I agree, counsel. The jury will disregard Senator Clay's attempt to cast a negative light on opposing counsel. Please avoid references to personal matters in the future.

**Clay:** I apologize to the Court, your Honor. I will proceed with my statement. People of the jury, as you heard Judge Williams say, it is our burden to prove beyond a shadow of a doubt that Senator Calhoun is guilty of treason to the United States. Therefore, we must show that he had some level of involvement in making war on our country. We must present two witnesses to testify that he did this. We feel strongly that we will be able to convince you of Senator Calhoun's guilt through compelling evidence and valid testimony from two reliable witnesses, one of them being the President of the United States, Andrew Jackson. (Pauses) This case stems from the Nullification Crisis that came to a head 3 years ago. We will show that John C. Calhoun incited his home state of South Carolina not only to nullify, or make void, legal acts passed by Congress, but he also incited that state to take up arms against our country. Armed conflict was only avoided because I proposed a compromise tariff bill in Congress. It was accepted, and war was averted. Now, I ask you people of the jury, what do you call an action of inciting a state to disobey a national law and inciting that state to increase its army and prepare for war against the rest of the country? I call it treason, and so will you when you have heard the testimony we will present.

(Sits at the prosecution table)

*Judge:* Does the defense have an opening statement?

*Hayne:* (Rising) We do, your Honor. (Stands before the jury) People of the jury, I suppose that I am at a disadvantage as opposing counsel has already attempted to introduce me, but let me add to his remarks with a more flattering description. My name is Robert Hayne, and I am currently the mayor of Charleston, SC. I have served my country and my state as a Captain in the Army during the War of 1812, as a Representative in the South Carolina Legislature, and as a Senator in the United States Congress. My co-counsel is Governor George McDuffie of South Carolina. He has served as a Representative in our state Legislature and in the United States Congress. Both of us have personal knowledge of the Nullification Crisis, as our state was the center of that event. Both of us know and understand that merely declaring a federal law destructive to a state is not at all an act of treason. Refusing to obey that law in the interest of a state is not an act of treason. Our evidence will show that even though Senator Calhoun supports the act of a state nullifying a federal law, he has never incited his home state to wage war against the United States. He has never committed treason. We are certain that as a fair-minded group of people, you the jury will find that Senator John C. Calhoun is a statesman of the highest order and contributes mightily to this nation. He does not attempt to destroy it. Thank you. (He sits at the defense table)

*Judge:* The prosecution will call its first witness.

*Webster:* (Rising) Your honor, we call President Andrew Jackson to the stand.

(Webster sits as Jackson comes forward and stands before the witness box while the clerk swears him in)

**Clerk:** Place your right hand on this Bible. Do you swear to tell the truth, the whole truth, and nothing but the truth?

**Jackson:** (With his hand on the Bible) I do. (Sits in the witness chair)

**Webster:** Please state your name and current occupation for the jury.

**Jackson:** My name is Andrew Jackson. I am the President of the United States.

**Webster:** Mr. President, have you had an occasion to know the defendant, Senator Calhoun?

**Jackson:** Yes, I've known the Senator for many years. He was my Vice President in my previous term of office.

**Webster:** But, he is not the Vice President during this term?

**Jackson:** No, he is not. He left that office to become a Senator.

**Webster:** Was there a reason left the Vice Presidency?

**Jackson:** Yes, there sure was. I don't associate with traitors.

**McDuffie:** (Rising) Objection! The witness is stating his opinion and slandering the defendant.

**Judge:** Objection sustained. Mr. President, please confine your remarks to facts, not opinions.

**Webster:** I'll rephrase the question. Mr. President, did there come a time when it seemed best that you and your Vice President should part ways? Did the Vice President actually resign from office?

**Jackson:** Yes, he resigned. For my next term of office I asked Martin Van Buren to run as Vice President.

**Webster:** Will you tell us about those circumstances, sir

**Jackson:** After Congress passed the Tariff of 1828, Mr. Calhoun was angry because he thought that the act highly favored the economy of the Northern states and significantly harmed the economy of the Southern states.

**Webster:** Do you have personal knowledge of this outlook by the defendant?

**Jackson:** Anybody who was within shouting distance had personal knowledge of his outlook. He ranted about it. He repeatedly called the act a Tariff of Abominations. Of course I had personal knowledge of it.

**Webster:** Was his being outspoken the reason you parted ways?

| Jackson: | No, anybody is entitled to an opinion even it's expressed too often and in an irritating manner. It's that secret document he wrote for the South Carolina Legislature that got me so stirred up. |
|---|---|
| Webster: | What document is that, Mr. President? |
| Jackson: | The "South Carolina Exhibition and Protest." |
| Webster: | Your Honor, may I introduce People's Exhibit A? It is an excerpt from the document in question. |
| Judge: | I'll allow it. |
| Webster: | (Stands and hands the document to the clerk who hands it to Jackson) Mr. President, will you please read the excerpt before you from the "South Carolina Exhibition and Protest"? |
| Jackson: | (Reading) " . . . if the system be persevered in, after due forbearance on the part of the State, that it will be her sacred duty to interpose her veto; a duty to herself, to the Union, to present, and to future generations, and to the cause of liberty over the world, to arrest the progress of a power . . . " |
| Webster: | Mr. President, what was your reaction when you read this statement? |
| Jackson: | It's obvious that the author, Calhoun, was calling for nullification of the Tariff Act and also calling for revolt if Congress didn't repeal the act. That business about arresting the progress of a power—the only way to do that is to fight. He was clearly threatening to literally fight the federal government if the tariff law held. That's one of the problems with nullification. If a state refuses to follow a federal law and the federal government challenges them on it, ultimately the state has only two choices: back down or secede. Secession is treason. |
| Webster: | Was there another occasion when you observed Mr. Calhoun diminish the United States? |
| Jackson: | Yes, there was. Many of us were gathered at an annual dinner honoring the memory of the great Thomas Jefferson. Someone asked me to make a toast for the occasion. I rose, looked squarely at John C. Calhoun and declared, "Our federal Union! It must be preserved!" |
| Webster: | What was the defendant's reaction to your toast? |
| Jackson: | Well, he stumbled around a minute, but he recovered himself to come back at me with his own declaration, "The Union, next to our liberty, most dear!" In front of this enormous crowd, Calhoun |

|  |  |
|---|---|
|  | confessed that the preservation of the United States was second to his state. I'm telling you, those are the words of a traitor! |
| McDuffie: | (Rising) Objection! The witness is slandering Senator Calhoun. |
| Judge: | Sustained! Mr. President, you will need to keep your opinions to yourself. I also consider your remarks an outburst, and I will not tolerate your making a soapbox of this court, even if you are the President of the United States. |
| Jackson: | I'm sorry, your Honor. It won't happen again. |
| Webster: | Mr. President, was there still another occasion when you came to question Senator Calhoun's loyalty to the United States? |
| Jackson: | Yes, there was. South Carolina did not directly act on the document the then Vice President wrote in secret. They merely published and circulated it as a pamphlet, which was damaging enough because it stirred people up. That was in 1828. But in 1832, Congress passed another tariff act thinking that it would soften the Tariff of 1828 and lessen the problems of the Southern states. But, South Carolina was angry about that tariff too. They held a convention and drew up a document called the South Carolina Ordinance of Nullification. That's when the situation reached the crisis level. |
| Webster: | Your Honor, may I enter Exhibit B for the people's case? It is an excerpt from the document passed by a special convention held in South Carolina on November 24, 1832, titled "South Carolina Ordinance of Nullification." |
| Judge: | You may. |
| Webster: | (Rises and hands the document to the clerk who hands it to Jackson) President Jackson, please read the passage before you. |
| Jackson: | (Reading) "And we, the people of South Carolina, to the end that it may be fully understood by the government of the United States, and the people of the co-States, that we are determined to maintain this our ordinance and declaration, at every hazard, do further declare that we will not submit to the application of force on the part of the federal government, to reduce this State to obedience . . . " |
| Webster: | How did you react to this document, Mr. President? |
| Jackson: | This passage comes near the end of the document, after it has declared the Tariff of 1832 null and void. This part of the ordinance threatens to meet force with force if the federal government took military measures to make South Carolina obey the law. Naturally, I had to respond to this drastic declaration. |

| | |
|---|---|
| *Webster:* | And, how did you do that, sir? |
| *Jackson:* | I issued a proclamation to the people of South Carolina appealing to their heritage of loyalty to the United States as exemplified by their courage in the Revolutionary War and the War of 1812. I told them this: "Disunion by armed force is treason." And, I asked them, "Are you really ready to incur its guilt?" |
| *Webster:* | What did you do to back up your proclamation? |
| *Jackson:* | I sent ships from the United States Navy to the Charleston Harbor. |
| *Webster:* | Did any military action take place? |
| *Jackson:* | No, Senator Clay came up with a compromise tariff bill in Congress, and that seemed to mollify the nullies. |
| *Webster:* | The nullies? |
| *Jackson:* | The people of South Carolina who were pushing nullification of the Tariff Act. |
| *Webster:* | And, was John C. Calhoun a nully? |
| *Jackson:* | Sir, he was the king of the nullies. |
| *Webster:* | I have no more questions for this witness. |
| *Judge:* | Very well. Does defense counsel wish to cross-examine? |
| *McDuffie:* | We do, your Honor. Mr. President, you seem to know the defendant quite well. |
| *Jackson:* | I'm sorry to say that I do. |
| *McDuffie:* | You've spent a great deal of time in his company? |
| *Jackson:* | More time than I care to remember. |
| *McDuffie:* | On any of these occasions did you ever hear him say that he was going to start a war against the United States? |
| *Jackson:* | No, I did not. |
| *McDuffie:* | Did you ever read a document where the defendant laid out a plan of attack against the United States? |
| *Jackson:* | No, I did not. |
| *McDuffie:* | So, President Jackson, you say that you know the defendant quite well, and you are sorry to say that you do. Could it be that you are testifying today because you have a personal grudge against Senator Calhoun? |
| *Jackson:* | No, that could not be. |
| *McDuffie:* | But, you do hold a grudge against the Senator? |

| Jackson: | I do not. |
| --- | --- |
| McDuffie: | Mr. President, aren't you still angry from the time you found out that in 1818 when the defendant was Secretary of War in President Monroe's Cabinet, he wrote a document urging censure against you for your invasion of Florida and the capture of Pensacola during the First Seminole War? |
| Jackson: | That was indeed a traitorous personal betrayal, but I do not hold a grudge, nor would I let that influence me in demonstrating the Senator's compunction for betraying his nation. |
| McDuffie: | But, you don't you take drastic action when you are angry? |
| Jackson: | I don't know what you mean or what that has to do with the relevance of this case. |
| McDuffie: | When you discovered that your Vice President had written the censure against you, what action did you take? |
| Jackson: | Action? Well, I no longer considered him to be a friend. I no longer considered him to be trustworthy. |
| McDuffie: | And? |
| Jackson: | And, I immediately removed Calhoun's cronies from my cabinet. |
| McDuffie: | So, you did retaliate against your Vice President? |
| Jackson: | I wouldn't call it retaliation. I would call it wisely preventing another act of betrayal. |
| McDuffie: | Let's move to another matter. Aren't you still angry with Senator Calhoun for his treatment of Mrs. Peggy Eaton? |
| Jackson: | If you are implying that I would accuse a man of the serious crime of treason to his country because his wife refused to invite my friend's wife to a party, you are seriously infringing on my character. I am against snobbery and hypocritical morality in all forms, but I am not a petty man, and I resent your implication that I am. |
| McDuffie: | So, Mr. President, do you deny that your testimony here today is a result of personal resentment against the defendant? |
| Jackson: | I deny that most vociferously. |
| McDuffie: | No further questions. |
| Judge: | Mr. President, you may step down. |

(Jackson leaves the court area)

| Judge: | Does the prosecution have another witness? |
|---|---|
| Webster: | (Rising) Yes, your Honor. We call Joel Roberts Poinsett to the stand. |

(Poinsett enters the court area and stands before the witness box. The clerk swears him in using the same procedure as with Jackson)

| Webster: | Please state your name and occupation for the jury. |
|---|---|
| Poinsett: | My name is Joel Roberts Poinsett, and I am currently a planter in South Carolina. |
| Webster: | But, you have also served your country in several capacities, haven't you? |
| Poinsett: | Yes, I have been in foreign service for the United States on missions in South America and Mexico. I have also served as a Representative in the United States Congress and in the South Carolina Legislature. |
| Webster: | You are a native of South Carolina? |
| Poinsett: | That is correct. |
| Webster: | Mr. Poinsett, are you not also a physician and something of a scientist? Botany, is it? |
| Poinsett: | That is true. Although I am a member of several science societies, I am but an amateur in fields other than medicine. |
| Webster: | That may be true, but haven't you had a plant named after you, one you brought from Mexico? |
| Poinsett: | I would not say that it is officially named after me at this point, but I believe that several people are working to have the beautiful plant I brought back from Mexico and grow in abundance on my plantation called a poinsettia. |
| Webster: | So, you are a man of vast experience with a deep interest in the politics and welfare of your country and of your state? |
| Poinsett: | I see myself this way, yes. |
| Webster: | Where were you when you heard that South Carolina was on the brink of calling a convention to nullify the Tariff of 1832? |
| Poinsett: | I was on an assignment in Mexico. |
| Webster: | What did you do at that time? |

| | |
|---|---|
| *Poinsett:* | I resigned my post and returned to South Carolina to try to persuade people in my state not go through with their plans to nullify the Tariff act. |
| *Webster:* | Why did you do this? |
| *Poinsett:* | I was alarmed for my state and for my country. If South Carolina maintained its threat to refuse to carry out the tariff law, then I knew military action would surely be the next step after officially declaring nullification. |
| *Webster:* | You said that you returned to persuade your state not to go through with the nullification. Did you have support for this effort? |
| *Poinsett:* | Oh, yes. Many of us Union Democrats took to the road. We covered South Carolina with our appeals. We wrote letters to newspapers, and we distributed pamphlets explaining the disasters of nullification. |
| *Webster:* | Did your attempts at persuading your state not to declare nullification of the tariff succeed? |
| *Poinsett:* | No, they did not. |
| *Webster:* | Mr. Poinsett, you stated that you were alarmed for your state. How alarmed were you and what steps did you take to meet that alarm? |
| *Poinsett:* | I consulted with President Jackson, and he authorized me to obtain arms and ammunition from the government's arsenal in Charleston. |
| *Webster:* | Why did you do this? |
| *Poinsett:* | I was concerned that because my state was building up its army, someone might try to seize the federal military stores in the harbor. |
| *Webster:* | So, you were concerned that war between South Carolina and the United States government could actually come about? |
| *Poinsett:* | I was quite concerned. Tempers were flaring. The atmosphere was heavy with danger. People were demonstrating by parading in the Charleston streets. Some of our citizens were spoiling for a fight. |
| *Webster:* | Mr. Poinsett, are you acquainted with the defendant, Senator John C. Calhoun? |
| *Poinsett:* | Yes, of course. He is quite revered in our state. Everyone knows who he is, and those of us in politics know him quite well. |
| *Webster:* | So, Senator Calhoun is highly respected in his state? |
| *Poinsett:* | Yes, the most highly respected. |

| | |
|---|---|
| *Webster:* | Would you say he has a great deal of influence in South Carolina? |
| *Poinsett:* | Absolutely. There's a saying in our state that goes, "When Calhoun takes snuff, South Carolina sneezes." |
| *Webster:* | Did he have very much influence in South Carolina regarding the Ordinance of Nullification? |
| *Poinsett:* | Of course. The convention that passed the Ordinance would never have met or declared nullification if Senator Calhoun had not instigated it. In fact, everyone called the concept "Calhoun's Doctrine of Nullification." |
| *Webster:* | (Rises) Your Honor, the people would like to enter Exhibit C into evidence at this time. |
| *Judge:* | Very, well, counselor. |
| *Webster:* | (Hands the object to the clerk who hands it to Poinsett) Mr. Poinsett, have you ever seen an object like this? |
| *Poinsett:* | (Examines the object) Oh, yes. These were circulated all over South Carolina during the Nullification Crisis. |
| *Webster:* | Will you identify the object and describe it for the jury? |
| *Poinsett:* | This is a medallion. It has an inscription that reads, "John C. Calhoun, First President of the Southern Confederacy." |
| *Webster:* | First President of the Southern Confederacy? What is the Southern Confederacy? |
| *Poinsett:* | It doesn't exist, but if South Carolina seceded from the United States and formed a new country, John C. Calhoun would not have an opponent in a presidential election. |
| *Webster:* | Does Senator Calhoun have aspirations of becoming president of a country that breaks away from the United States? |
| *Poinsett:* | Well, if he doesn't, a lot of other people sure have aspirations for him. |
| *Webster:* | No more questions. |
| *Judge:* | Does the defense wish to cross-examine the witness? |
| *McDuffie:* | (Rising) We do, you Honor. (Sits down) Mr. Poinsett, have you ever heard Senator Calhoun declare war against the United States? |
| *Poinsett:* | No, I have not. |
| *McDuffie:* | Have you ever seen written plans or plots that the Senator has made for bearing arms against the United States? |
| *Poinsett:* | No, I have not. |

| | |
|---|---|
| *McDuffie:* | Do you have personal knowledge that the defendant has taken overt steps to make war against the United States? |
| *Poinsett:* | No, I have not. |
| *McDuffie:* | I have no further questions for this witness. |
| *Judge:* | Mr. Poinsett, you may step down. |

(Poinsett leaves the court area)

| | |
|---|---|
| *Judge:* | Does the Prosecution have another witness? |
| *Webster:* | We have no more witnesses, your Honor. The Prosecution rests. |
| *Judge:* | Very well. Will the Defense call your first witness? |
| *Hayne:* | (Rising) Yes, your Honor. The Defense calls Senator John C. Calhoun. |

(Calhoun rises, stands before the witness box while the clerk swears him in, and sits in the witness chair)

| | |
|---|---|
| *McDuffie:* | Sir, please state your name and current occupation. |
| *Calhoun:* | My name is John Caldwell Calhoun, and I am currently serving as a United States Senator from South Carolina. |
| *McDuffie:* | Haven't you served your country in other capacities, as well as Senator? |
| *Calhoun:* | Yes. I have been a Representative in the United States Congress, Vice President of the United States during the terms of Presidents John Quincy Adams and Andrew Jackson, and Secretary of War in the Cabinet of President James Monroe. |
| *McDuffie:* | Do you then consider yourself loyal to your country? |
| *Calhoun:* | I am a true patriot, Sir. |
| *McDuffie:* | Have you ever conspired to make war against the United States or taken military action toward the United States? |
| *Calhoun:* | No, I have not. |
| *McDuffie:* | Now about this nullification business, do you consider nullification an act of treason? |
| *Calhoun:* | No, I do not. I consider nullification an alternative to secession and therefore a means of avoiding secession and inevitable military conflict. If a state nullifies a federal act, it merely concentrates on |

that one act. That state is exercising its natural right to protect itself against whatever harm that federal act may cause. It is not making military threats.

McDuffie: Can you cite a precedent for nullification as means of a state exercising its natural rights?

Calhoun: The Kentucky and Virginia Resolutions authored by our revered statesmen Thomas Jefferson and James Madison are solid documents that proposed nullification.

McDuffie: Will you explain to the jury the circumstances and content of the Kentucky and Virginia Resolutions?

Calhoun: Actually these were two separate sets of resolutions. The legislatures of Kentucky and Virginia both passed their declarations to ignore the Alien and Sedition Acts passed by the United States Congress. These declarations were acts of nullification. In both cases, the states were against the federal government taking action against citizens within their states.

McDuffie: What was especially significant about these two documents?

Calhoun: They made it clear that the United States Constitution is a compact among the states. If a state regards a certain federal law as being against the Constitution, the state does not need to accept that act as law within its state.

McDuffie: What gives a state this right?

Calhoun: The Constitution gives this right. It states that certain powers are reserved for the states. Therefore, the states have a right to determine the constitutionality of a federal law.

McDuffie: So, you believe that the act of nullification is a right that belongs to the states?

Calhoun: I do.

McDuffie: And, you do not see nullification as a step toward secession or toward making war on the United States?

Calhoun: I see nullification as a way to help a minority protect itself against a majority that has no interest or concern for the consequences of an action that harms the affected minority. Nullification is a means of allowing all parties to have the best outcome for their circumstances.

McDuffie: Senator, have you ever incited the state of South Carolina to take treasonous steps toward the United States?

| | |
|---|---|
| Calhoun: | No, I have not. |
| McDuffie: | Have you ever made war or been part of plan or a group of people planning to make war on the United States? |
| Calhoun: | No, I have not, and I never will. |
| McDuffie: | I have no further questions for this witness. |
| Judge: | Does the prosecution wish to cross-examine the witness? |
| Webster: | (Rises) We do, you Honor. (Sits) Senator Calhoun, are you aware of other state's reactions to the Kentucky and Virginia Resolutions? |
| Calhoun: | Yes, I am. |
| Webster: | What was New Hampshire's reaction? |
| Calhoun: | That state passed a resolution to defend the Constitution against all foreign and domestic aggression against the United States. |
| Webster: | So, that state considered Kentucky and Virginia's declarations of nullification as aggressive acts? |
| Calhoun: | It would appear so. |
| Webster: | What did that resolution say about the right of a state to treat a federal law as unconstitutional? |
| Calhoun: | That document stated that it was not the privilege of a state legislature to declare a federal law unconstitutional. They said the power to do this was strictly with the federal judicial department. |
| Webster: | And, doesn't the Constitution give the judicial department this power? |
| Calhoun: | Yes, it does, but it also reserves powers to the states. |
| Webster: | So, you disagree with the New Hampshire resolution? |
| Calhoun: | Most definitely. |
| Webster: | Senator Calhoun, how many other southern states joined South Carolina in nullifying the Tariff Act of 1832? |
| Calhoun: | None. |
| Webster: | In fact, didn't Louisiana pass a resolution condemning South Carolina's Ordinance of Nullification and professing loyalty to President Jackson's firm stand against your state's action? |
| Calhoun: | Yes. |
| Webster: | And, wasn't part of the President's firm stand that the act of nullification is treasonous? |

| | |
|---|---|
| **Calhoun:** | That seems to be the President's opinion, his very personal opinion. |
| **Webster:** | But, you do not see nullification as a prelude to secession or war? |
| **Calhoun:** | No, I do not. |
| **Webster:** | How do your explain the fact that your state simultaneously increased the build-up of its army with the passing of the Ordinance of Nullification? |
| **Calhoun:** | I do not know. You would have to ask the framers of those documents. |
| **Webster:** | Senator Calhoun, have you ever attempted to run for President of the United States? |
| **McDuffie:** | (Rises) Objection! How can the Senator's political aspirations have any bearing on the issues of this case? |
| **Judge:** | Counselor, do you intend to show relevance to your question? |
| **Webster:** | I do, your Honor. |
| **Judge:** | Very well. The objection is overruled. However, Senator Webster, I expect you to connect this line of questioning to the case immediately. |
| **Webster:** | Thank you, your Honor. Senator Calhoun, did you ever attempt to run for President of the Untied States? |
| **Calhoun:** | I considered it. |
| **Webster:** | You have been Vice President under two Presidents. Why didn't you run for President? |
| **Calhoun:** | I lacked the support I needed. |
| **Webster:** | Did you expect that being Vice President during President Jackson's term of office would eventually propel you the presidency? |
| **Calhoun:** | That decision is in the hands of the voters. |
| **Webster:** | But, did you hope that the position would give you that opportunity, especially if President Jackson endorsed you? |
| **Calhoun:** | I can't answer that. |
| **Webster:** | And then, when you broke with the President and he chose Martin Van Buren as his Vice President, didn't it become clear that you would never ascend to the presidency? And, didn't this kill your ultimate political ambitions? |
| **McDuffie:** | (Rising) Objection! Counsel is badgering the witness. |

**Judge:** Sustained, and Senator Webster, it is time for you make the point you promised the court a few minutes ago.

**Webster:** Yes, your Honor. Senator Calhoun, have you seen this medallion, People's Exhibit C?

(The clerk gives Calhoun the medallion)

**Calhoun:** Yes, of course I've seen many of these medallions. They are all over South Carolina.

**Webster:** Please read the inscription.

**Calhoun:** "John C. Calhoun: First President of the Southern Confederacy."

**Webster:** Did you order these medallions to be struck and distributed in your state?

**Calhoun:** Of course not.

**Webster:** What is the Southern Confederacy?

**Calhoun:** It does not exist.

**Webster:** Would you like for it to exist?

**Calhoun:** Certainly not.

**Webster:** Isn't it true that if you cannot become President of the United States, you would attempt to create a new country that would elect you as President?

**McDuffie:** (Rising) Objection!

**Webster:** Your Honor, I have no further questions of this witness.

**Judge:** Senator Calhoun, you may step down. Does the defense have another witness?

**McDuffie:** (Rises) We do, your Honor. We call James Hamilton, Jr. to the stand. (Sits)

(Hamilton stands in front of the witness box while the clerk swears him in and then sits in the witness seat)

**McDuffie:** Please state your name and current occupation for the court.

**Hamilton:** My name is James Hamilton. I am currently living in Texas and, as a lawyer I am assisting the good citizens there in negotiating with the Mexican government for Texas to receive their independence from Mexico.

| | |
|---|---|
| *McDuffie:* | Have you served in public capacities in the United States? |
| *Hamilton:* | Yes, I served as a major in the United States Army during the War of 1812. I have held seats in both houses of the South Carolina Legislature and I have been a Representative from South Carolina in the United States Congress. I have also been Governor of South Carolina. |
| *McDuffie:* | Were you governor when the convention met to pass the Ordinance of Nullification? |
| *Hamilton:* | Yes, I presided over that convention. |
| *McDuffie:* | Did you call that convention? |
| *Hamilton:* | Yes, I did. |
| *McDuffie:* | Was the purpose of that convention to officially secede from the United States? |
| *Hamilton:* | Absolutely not. |
| *McDuffie:* | What was the purpose of the convention? |
| *Hamilton:* | Our purpose was to determine if South Carolina felt the need to officially declare nullification of the Tariffs of 1828 and 1832. It had absolutely nothing to do with secession. |
| *McDuffie:* | And, did the delegates at the convention vote to nullify the tariff act? |
| *Hamilton:* | Yes, they did. They voted to pass the South Carolina Ordinance of Nullification, November 24, 1832. |
| *McDuffie:* | What were the terms of the ordinance? |
| *Hamilton:* | South Carolina would not abide by any of the terms of the two tariff acts in question. |
| *McDuffie:* | When was the ordinance scheduled to go into effect? |
| *Hamilton:* | February 1, 1833. We wanted to give Congress time to rescind the acts. |
| *McDuffie:* | Did South Carolina carry out the ordinance? |
| *Hamilton:* | No, it wasn't necessary. Congress did pass a new tariff law that was acceptable to the state of South Carolina. |
| *McDuffie:* | During this time now referred to as the Nullification Crisis, did South Carolina increase the state's army? |
| *Hamilton:* | Yes, we did that. |
| *McDuffie:* | And, what was the purpose of this increase? |

| | |
|---|---|
| Hamilton: | We knew that in declaring nullification of the tariff laws, we would possibly have to defend ourselves in order to carry it out. President Jackson had made strong threats against our state if we took actual steps to enact our procedures to go against the tariff acts. |
| McDuffie: | But, you did not plan to be the aggressor? |
| Hamilton: | No, we did not. We simply prepared to defend ourselves. |
| McDuffie: | Mr. Hamilton, you know the defendant John C. Calhoun quite well, don't you? |
| Hamilton: | I am pleased to have this great statesman as a close and personal friend. |
| McDuffie: | So, you have had many conversations with him? |
| Hamilton: | Yes, I have. |
| McDuffie: | And, you have corresponded with the defendant? |
| Hamilton: | Yes, I have. |
| McDuffie: | In any of these conversations or correspondences, did the defendant ever discuss plans to overthrow the government of the United States? |
| Hamilton: | No, he did not. |
| McDuffie: | Did he ever reveal plans to make war against the United States? |
| Hamilton: | No, he did not. |
| McDuffie: | Have you ever seen him take military action against the United States? |
| Hamilton: | No, I have not. |
| McDuffie: | I have no more questions for this witness. |
| Judge: | Does the prosecution wish to cross-examine? |
| Webster: | (Rises) We do, your Honor. (Sits) Mr. Hamilton, you were in the thick of the Nullification Crisis, weren't you? |
| Hamilton: | I beg your pardon? |
| Webster: | You called a convention to nullify the tariff acts, and you presided over that convention, didn't you? |
| Hamilton: | Yes, I did. That was my duty as governor of South Carolina at that time. |
| Webster: | In fact, you have publicly and frequently proclaimed your firm beliefs in states' rights and nullification, haven't you? |
| Hamilton: | Yes, I have. |

| | |
|---|---|
| *Webster:* | And, in this Ordinance of Nullification, you made provisions for a build up of your state's army. Isn't that correct? |
| *Hamilton:* | Yes, as I explained earlier, we needed to prepare for President Jackson's threatened aggression against South Carolina. |
| *Webster:* | Did you receive a high command in this new organization of South Carolina's army? |
| *Hamilton:* | Yes, I was Brigadier General of our state's army. |
| *Webster:* | Were you prepared to secede from the Union if you deemed it necessary? |
| *Hamilton:* | No, I have never supported secession and I have never urged secession. |
| *Webster:* | Will you please examine the medallion the clerk will give you at this time? |
| *Hamilton:* | Yes, of course. |

(The clerk hands the medallion to Hamilton)

| | |
|---|---|
| *Webster:* | Mr. Hamilton, have you seen this medallion before? |
| *Hamilton:* | Yes, I have. |
| *Webster:* | Will you please read the inscription on it? |
| *Hamilton:* | "John C. Calhoun: First President of the Southern Confederacy." |
| *Webster:* | Did you order copies of this medallion to be struck and circulated, sir? |
| *Hamilton:* | No, I did not. |
| *Webster:* | Do you know who did? |
| *Hamilton:* | No, I do not. |
| *Webster:* | Did John C. Calhoun order copies of this medallion to be struck and circulated? |
| *Hamilton:* | No, he did not. |
| *Webster:* | You testified that you did not know who gave the order. |
| *Hamilton:* | That is correct. |
| *Webster:* | Then, you don't know who gave the order? |
| *Hamilton:* | No, I do not. |
| *Webster:* | So, isn't it true that the defendant could have given the order, but you wouldn't have necessarily known that? |

| | |
|---|---|
| *Hamilton:* | I'm confident that he did not give the order. |
| *Webster:* | I have no further questions of this witness. |
| *Judge:* | Very well. The witness may step down. Does the defense have another witness? |
| *McDuffie:* | No, your Honor. The defense rests. |
| *Judge:* | Is the prosecution ready to present your closing statement? |
| *Clay:* | (Rises) We are, your honor. (Stands before the jury) People of the jury, the prosecution has been given the task of proving beyond a shadow of a doubt that John C. Calhoun is guilty of treason against the United States. According to our Constitution, we needed to show that the defendant has levied war against the United States. We also needed to produce two witnesses to testify to that deed. Did John C. Calhoun pickup a weapon and actively lead a charge against a United States military fortress? No, but he has incited others to secede from this country. Secession is surely an act of war. He has written secret documents encouraging citizens to disobey the laws of this nation. Through public orations and a heavy distribution of publications, he has openly incited the people of his state to go against their country. He has stirred up the people of South Carolina so that they passed an official Ordinance of Nullification and raised an army. Both of these actions defy their country, and both are acts of war. The evidence of this cancerous discontent among the people of South Carolina resides in this abominable medallion. (Passes the medallion to circulate among the jurors) The inscription reading, "John C. Calhoun: First President of the Southern Confederacy" tells us that this man has gone beyond inciting people to take military action. He has incited them to create a new country and even give it a name. This medallion alone is enough to convict John C. Calhoun of treason, but our Constitution says that we must also produce two witnesses, and we have done so. The President of the United States, Andrew Jackson, recognized treason in the secret document John C. Calhoun wrote while serving as Vice President of the United States. Surely the defendant himself recognized his act as traitorous because he wrote the "South Carolina Exposition and Protest" document in secret. Why did he not make this document public? Further, President Jackson personally heard the defendant make a toast in a public gathering placing personal liberty above his country. Then, at the defendant's instigation, the State of South Carolina passed the Ordinance of Nullification and immediately prepared itself for war against the United States. |

As a witness, President Jackson testified to this military build-up and threat from that state because he saw fit to send naval ships to the Charleston harbor to use if necessary to force South Carolina to obey federal laws. No other state has chosen to support South Carolina in this treasonous stance. In fact, the state of Louisiana passed a resolution condemning South Carolina's Ordinance of Nullification and declaring full loyalty to our President and his actions to stop the ordinance of nullification from being enacted. Now, the Constitution says that we needed to produce a second witness, and we have done so in the person of Mr. Joel Roberts Poinsett. This gentleman was so alarmed when he heard that his state was on the brink of officially declaring nullification of a federal law, he resigned his post of service in Mexico and returned to South Carolina to meet the crisis. He and many other Union Democrats of South Carolina tried to reason with the people of his state not to call a nullification convention and not to pass an ordinance of nullification. But, the people of this state were so stirred up by John C. Calhoun that their efforts failed. Then Mr. Poinsett became so alarmed that his state would take military action against the United States, that he gained permission from President Jackson to seize military stores belonging to the federal government before the state troops could do so. People of the jury, the pall of treason has blanketed South Carolina and smothered it with this terrible crime. And, who hurled this blanket over the people of that state? You know who it was. You know it was John C. Calhoun. People of the jury, we have exposed the treasonous acts of John C. Calhoun. And, we have supplied two valid witnesses. Do not be deceived by the aura of reason the defendant has cloaked himself in for this trial. We have exposed to you a man "with too much genius and too little common sense, who will either die a traitor or a madman." It is up to you to decide which course he will take. It is your duty to find the defendant, John C. Calhoun, guilty of treason.

(Clay sits at the prosecution table)

Judge:  Does the defense have a closing statement?

Hayne:  (Rises) We do, your Honor. (Stands in front of the jury) People of the jury, today you have not heard testimony proving a charge of treason. You have heard slander. You have heard Senator Calhoun who has served his country in many capacities called a traitor. But, you have not heard that he committed a traitorous act. You have not heard anyone say that John C. Calhoun has taken steps to make war against his country. The United States Constitution says that two witnesses must testify that they have knowledge of a person levying war against our country. The prosecution has produced two witnesses, but let's look not only at what they have said, but even more telling, what they have not said. Let's also look at who they are. President Jackson appears to feel slighted that Senator Calhoun wrote a secret document when he was Vice President under President Jackson. Is that treason? Absolutely not! President Jackson appears to feel slighted because Senator Calhoun wrote a proposal to censure his actions in Florida as long ago as 1818. Could this be why the President is so inclined to testify against the defendant in 1835? Has he been carrying a personal grudge against John C. Calhoun all of these years and now he finally sees a way to publicly humiliate the defendant? Or, could the President have found a way to avenge his friend John Eaton because Mrs. Calhoun refused to invite Mr. Eaton's wife to a Washington party? It is public knowledge that President Jackson became enraged over this apparent snub. We are searching for the reason for his willingness to testify because he has nothing to offer about the charge of treason against Senator Calhoun. He has not heard the defendant say anything, nor has he seen the defendant take any action against his country. Therefore, his testimony is invalid. The second witness is Joel Roberts Poinsett, who is poised on the brink of having a plant named in his honor. This is hardly a qualification for making sound judgments about the serious matter of treason. Again, this witness might be seizing what he perceives as an opportunity to publicly humiliate the defendant. John C. Calhoun is a highly respected statesman in South Carolina. Mr. Poinsett is affiliated with the Union Democratic Party, so he is of a different political philosophy than Senator Calhoun. During the nullification crisis, Mr. Poinsett and his associates tried to persuade the good people of South Carolina that nullification was the wrong course of action for that state to endorse. Mr. Poinsett's faction failed. Those who supported Senator Calhoun's ideas succeeded. Could Mr. Poinsett now think that he has found a way to strike at his nemesis? Joel Roberts Poinsett has not testified that he has seen or heard John C. Calhoun making or carrying out treasonous plans against the United States. Therefore, he is also an invalid witness. So, who among the witnesses is valid? Certainly Mr. Hamilton is acceptable because he has been in Senator Calhoun's company on many occasions and has frequently corresponded with the defendant, and he has never seen or heard of the senator taking treasonous steps against the United States. That leaves us to analyze the testimony of John C. Calhoun, the man who best knows his own intentions. Does he believe that nullification is a treasonous act? No, this statesman has testified that he offered nullification as a peaceful alternative to secession by his state. He has found a way for the minority to avoid suffering from actions taken by the majority. In the Tariff Acts of 1828 and 1832, the minority suffered economically while the majority gained economically. Senator Calhoun has offered a way for both parties to gain. Let the majority abide by the Tariff Acts, and let the minority disregard the Tariff Acts. People of the jury, this is an act of unification, not an act of separation. John C. Calhoun is a unifier, not a traitor. I trust that you will acknowledge his qualifications as a true and loyal statesman of his country by finding him not guilty.

(Hayne sits at the defense table)

**Judge:**    Thank you, counselors. And, thank you people of the jury for your attentive service. Now it is time for me to charge the jury. People of the jury, here is your charge: After due deliberation, you must return a verdict that John C. Calhoun is either guilty or not guilty of treason against the United States. Your verdict must reflect your understanding of the definition of treason according to the United States Constitution. If you find the defendant guilty, you must do so beyond a reasonable doubt. You may begin your deliberations.

## SOURCES:

*An outline of American History: Nullification crisis.* Available from http://www. let.rug.nl/~usa/H/1994/ch5_p5.htm. Accessed 4 June 2007.

Bennett, B. *Preserving our federal union.* Available from http://www.townhall. com/columnists/BillBennett/2006/05/23/preserving_our_federal_ union. Accessed 4 June 2007. ·

*John C. Calhoun.* Available from http://en.wikipedia.org/wiki/John_C._ Calhoun. Accessed 4 June 2007.

*John C. Calhoun: A brief introduction.* Available from http://xroads.virginia. edu/~cap/CALHOUN/jcc1.html. Accessed 4 June 2007.

*Nullification proclamation.* Available from http://www.loc.gov/rr/ program/bib/ourdocs/Nullification.html. Accessed 4 June 2007.

*President Jackson's proclamation regarding nullification, December 10, 1832.* Available from http://www.yale.edu/lawweb/avalon/presiden/proclamations/jack01. htm. Accessed 4 June 2007.

Rossman, T. S., & Benson, T. L. *The address.* Available from http://facweb. furman.edu/~benson/docs/calhoun.htm. Accessed 4 June 2007.

*South Carolina governors—George McDuffie, 1834–1836.* Available from http://sciway.net/hist/governors/mcduffie.html. Accessed 4 June 2007.

*South Carolina governors—Stephen Decatur Miller, 1828–1830.* Available from http://sciway.net/hist/governors/miller.html. Accessed 4 June 2007.

*South Carolina Ordinance of Nullification, November 24, 1832.* Available from http://elsinore.cis.yale.edu/lawweb/avalon/states/sc/ordnull.htm. Accessed 4 June 2007.

Thompson, E. M. *Joel Roberts Poinsett: The man behind the flower.* Available from http://owmg.org/Education/STB/STB-1984/STB-DE84.txt. Accessed 4 June 2007.

*Virtual American biographies: Joel Roberts Poinsett.* Available from http:// famousamericans.net/joelrobertspoinsett. Accessed 4 June 2007.

# References

*An outline of American History: Nullification crisis.* (1994). Retrieved June 4, 2007, from http://www.let.rug.nl/~usa/H/1994/ch5_p5.htm

Bennett, B. (2006). *Preserving our federal union.* Retrieved June 4, 2007, from http://www.townhall.com/columnists/BillBennett/2006/05/23/preserving_our_federal_union

*Bob Hope and American variety.* (2004). Retrieved March 10, 2006, from http://www.loc.gov/exhibits/bobhope/uso.html

Bray, W. (1958). *Everyday life of the Aztecs.* New York: Dorset Press.

Bull, A. (2000). *Joan of Arc.* New York: DK Publishing.

Chestnut, M. B. M. (1997). *A diary from Dixie.* Retrieved October 16, 2005, from http://docsouth.unc.edu/southlit/chesnut/maryches.html#mches21 (Original work published 1861)

Connaughton, J. (2001). *The big ski nose meets the big tail bird.* Retrieved March 10, 2006, from http://home.att.net/~ww2aviation/BobHope.html

Davis, K. C. (1990). *Don't know much about history.* New York: Crown Publishers.

Davison, M. W. (Ed.). (1993). *When, where, why, and how it happened.* London: Reader's Digest.

Deaton, D. (2003). *Famous entertainers brought hope, cheer to Percy Jones.* Retrieved March 10, 2006, from http://www.dlis.dla.mil/FederalCenter/Releases/story030414.asp

*George Washington, 1789–1797.* (n. d.). Retrieved May 15, 2007, from http://www.kipnotes.com/GeorgeWashington.htm

Ifill, G. (2001). *Conversation: Jimmy Carter.* Retrieved January 12, 2005, from http://www.pbs.org/newshour/conversation/jan-june01/carter_01-10.html

*Jefferson's letter.* (n. d.). Retrieved December 12, 2006, from http://lewisandclarktrail.com/legacy/letter.htm.

*Joan of Arc.* (n. d.). Retrieved May 10, 2007, from http://en.wikipedia.org/wiki/Joan_of_Arc

*John C. Calhoun.* (n. d.). Retrieved June 4, 2007, from http://en.wikipedia.org/wiki/John_C._Calhoun

*John C. Calhoun: A brief introduction.* (n. d.). Retrieved June 4, 2007, from http://xroads.virginia.edu/~cap/CALHOUN/jcc1.html

Krull, K. (2004). *A woman for president: The story of Victoria Woodhull.* New York: Walker and Company.

Lange, K. (2007). *What would you take to the New World?* Retrieved May 15, 2007, from http://www7.nationalgeographic.com/ngm/0705/feature2/index.html

*Letters from the GIs.* (n. d.). Retrieved March 10, 2006 from http://www.bobhope.com/bhletters.html

*Nullification proclamation.* (n. d.). Retrieved June 4, 2007, from http://www.loc.gov/rr/program/bib/ourdocs/Nullification.html

*President Jackson's proclamation regarding nullification, December 10, 1832.* (1999). Retrieved June 4, 2007, from http://www.yale.edu/lawweb/avalon/presiden/proclamations/jack01.htm (Original work published 1832)

Rossman, T. S., & Benson, T. L. (n. d.). *The address.* Retrieved June 4, 2007, from http://facweb.furman.edu/~benson/docs/calhoun.htm (Original work printed 1851)

*South Carolina governors—George McDuffie, 1834–1836.* (n. d.). Retrieved June 4, 2007, from http://sciway.net/hist/governors/mcduffie.html

*South Carolina governors—Stephen Decatur Miller, 1828–1830.* (n. d.). Retrieved June 4, 2007, from http://sciway.net/hist/governors/miller.html

*South Carolina Ordinance of Nullification, November 24, 1832.* (1999). Retrieved June 4, 2007, from http://elsinore.cis.yale.edu/lawweb/avalon/states/sc/ordnull.htm (Original work published 1832)

*Taj Mahal impressions.* (n. d.). Retrieved June 4, 2007, from http://www.taj-mahal-india-travel.com/impressions-of-taj-mahal-india.html

Thompson, E. M. (1984). *Joel Roberts Poinsett: The man behind the flower.* Retrieved June 4, 2007, from http://owmg.org/Education/STB/STB-1984/STB-DE84.txt

Turabian, K. (1996). *A manual for writers of term papers, theses, and dissertations* (6th ed.). Chicago: The University of Chicago Press.

*Virtual American biographies: Joel Roberts Poinsett.* (2000). Retrieved June 4, 2007, from http://famousamericans.net/joelrobertspoinsett

# About the Author

**H**elen Bass, a retired history and English teacher, has conducted history fairs at several levels of competition. She has also served as social studies specialist for Education Service Center Region VI in Huntsville, TX, and as a staff developer of the Texas Social Studies Center for the Texas Education Agency.

She has written social studies materials for teachers and conducted workshops for educators throughout Texas and across the United States. Bass has received the Leon Jaworski Award for Texas teachers who teach law-related education in secondary schools.

As a social studies consultant, she continues to promote innovative learning by assisting teachers in developing vibrant history experiences for their students.